TEACH YOURSELF URDU

IN TWO MONTHS

ا ب ت ث ج ح خ د ذ ر ز

س ص ض ط ظ ع غ ف ک ق ل

م ن و ہ ھ لا ء ی ے

Prof. 'Aziz-ur-Rahman

www.idaraimpex.com

TEACH YOURSELF
URDU IN TWO MONTHS

Prof. 'Aziz-ur-Rahman

9788171011865 00000

ISBN: 81-7101-186-1

Edition: 2012

TP-278-14

Published by Mohammad Yunus for

IDARA IMPEX

D-80, Abul Fazal Enclave-I, Jamia Nagar
New Delhi-110 025 (India)
Tel.: +91-11-2695 6832 & 085888 33786
Fax: +91-11-6617 3545 Email: **sales@idara.co**
Online Store: **www.idarastore.com**

Retail Shop:

IDARA IMPEX

Shop 6, Nizamia Complex, Gali Gadrian, Hazrat Nizamuddin
New Delhi-110013 (India) Tel.: 085888 44786

CONTENTS

PART I

PART II

PART III

THE NOUN

PART IV

VERBS FOLLOWING PARTICULAR RULES

PART V

USES OF SOME PARTICULAR WORDS

PART VI

NARRATIVES STORIES FOR TRANSLATION

PART VII

USEFUL SENTENCES

PART VIII

VOCABULARY

PREFACE

The chief object of this book is to meet a beignner's wants, and to remove the difficults, which are not explained in most other books.

Points which to a learned writer may seem too easy to require an explanation, often present a great difficulty to a beginner.

When starting to learn Urdu a beginner has to face several difficulties, *e.g.*,

(i) The pronunciation;

(ii) The order of words in a sentence;

(iii) Formation of the various plurals;

(iv) Agreement of the Adjective and Verbs with the Nouns in gender, number and case.

Now, if a beginner (of elementary education) is taught and expected to observe all the above rules at the very beginning, he naturally gets confused, and regards the language as too tedious to be learnt and gives it up as a failure.

During his 30 years' experience, the author had come to the conclusion that it is best to master one difficulty at a time, in particular the art of putting words in the right order, otherwise the agreement of words will be confused.

The following rules have been observed in this book,

(1) The second chapter teaches only the order of words in a sentence. The beginner, having mastered the rule, can then confidently proceed with the grammar.

(2) In order to refresh the student's memory, the English grammer terms are explained as they occur in the book.

(3) Under each sentence, in the examples, the English words are put in the order in which they are to be translated into Urdu.

(4) The examples to every rule are arranged, in such a way that, if carefully studied, they will answer any question which may arise in the mind of a student, when doing the exercise concerned.

(5) Under each rule two exercise are given, one to be translated from Urdu into English, and the other from English into Urdu.

(6) After every five or six rules, revisional exercises, composed of mixed sentences on the preceding rules, are given to ensure that the student remembers those rules before he proceeds any further.

In short, neither effort nor pain has been spared to make this book clear, useful, and as simple as possible. To ensure this, each rule in the book has been successfully tried on a considerable number of promising pupils, while studying under the author.

In conclusion, I wish to thank those who have patronized and shown appreciation of my humble efforts in producing this book.

Aziz-ur-Rahman

بِسْمِ اللّٰہِ الرَّحْمٰنِ الرَّحِیْمِ

Bismil-la-hir-Rahman-ir-Raheem

I begin this work in the name of Allah, the Beneficent, the Merciful.

PART 1

URDU ALPHABETS AND SYSTEM OF TRANSLITERATION

Urdu, like Persian and Arabic, is written from right to left and the letters consist of strokes or strokes and dots. At the end of a word or when standing alone many letters end with a flourish. Learners should, first of all, try to acquire a complete mastery over the 'Detached Form' of the Alphabet. Those desirous of speaking only should start the book from page 17. For pronunciation, however, they will have to refer to the following chart and 'Guide to Pronunciation' on Page 7.

Name	Detached Form	Transliteration and Pronunciation	
Alif	ا	A.	as A in far
Bē	ب	B.	as in English
Pē	پ	P.	as in English
Tē	ت	T.	a soft dental like in three
Tē	ٹ	T.	hard as T in Tin—tack
Sē	ث	S.	as S in sit
Jeem	ج	J.	like J in Jail
Chē	چ	Ch.	like Ch in Church
Hē	ح	H.	like H in Huge
Khē	خ	Kh	guttural, as Ch in I och
Dāl	د	D.	soft, as Th in Thee
Dāl	ڈ	D.	hard, as D in Dog
Zāl	ذ	Z.	like Z in Zeal
Rē	ر	R	as in English
Rē	ڑ	Re,	a hard R
Zē	ز	Z.	as in English
Zhē	ژ	Zh.	as in Azure
Seen	س	S	like S in. Sit

Name	Detached Form	Transliteration and Pronunciation	
Sheen	ش	Sh.	as Sh in Shut
Suād	ص	S.	as S in Sit
Zuād	ض	Z.	as Z in Zeal
Toē	ط	T.	as T in Tie
Zoē	ظ	Z.	as Z in Zeal
Ain	ع	A.	gutteral (consonant)
Ghain	غ	Gh.	as G in the German word Segen.
Fē	ف	F.	as F in Fun
Quaf	ق	Q.	gutteral, like Ch in Stuck
Kāf	ک	K.	as in English
Gāf	گ	G.	as G in Give
Lām	ل	L.	as L in Lane
Meem	م	M.	as in English
Noon	ن	N.	as in English
Wāo	و	W.	O. U. as in English
Hē	ہ	H.	as H in Hot
Yē	ی	Y.	as Y in yad
Yē	ے	E.	as Ey in They

DIFFERENT FORMS OF LETTERS

All letters, with a few exceptions, have four forms, i.e. initial, medial, final and independent. The independent form is also called 'the Detached Form'. To write a word all the ltters used are joined to one another. The essential part of the ltter, however, remains unchanged as is shown here :—

Detached form	initial	medial	final
ب	بـ	ـبـ	ـب

Detached Form

ا ب پ ت ٹ ث

ج چ ح خ د ڈ ذ

ر ڑ ز ژ س ش

ص ض ط ظ ع غ

ف ق ک گ ل م ن

و ہ ی ے

INITIAL FORM

To obtain the initial form strike off the horizontal lines and circles of the detached form, as,

بـ پـ تـ ٹـ ثـ جـ چـ حـ خـ

سـ شـ صـ ضـ طـ ظـ عـ غـ

فـ قـ کـ گـ لـ مـ نـ ہـ یـ

IMPORTANT : Since the following nine ltters have neither a circle nor a horizontal line they do not change except in the case of the final form. They are always joined to the preceding letter but not to the one following. All letters when used after them are written in the initial or detached form as the case may be.

ا د ڈ ذ ر ڑ ز ژ و

MEDIAL FORM

The medial form is obtained by adding a connecting line to the right side of the initial form, as.

ـبـ ـپـ ـتـ ـٹـ ـثـ ـجـ ـچـ ـحـ ـخـ

ـسـ ـشـ ـصـ ـضـ ـطـ ـظـ ـعـ ـغـ

ـفـ ـقـ ـکـ ـگـ ـلـ ـمـ ـنـ ـھـ ـیـ

FINAL FORM

The final form is obtained by adding the same connecting line to the beginning of the detached form.

ـا ـب ـپ ـت ـٹ ـث ـج ـچ

ـح ـخ ـد ـڈ ـذ ـر ـڑ ـز ـژ ـس ـش

ـص ـض ـط ـظ ـع ـغ ـف

ـق ـک ـگ ـل ـم ـن ـو ـہ ـی ـے

Exercise 1(a)

Read and copy the following words:

sab سب سـ ب jab جب جـ ب	bas بس بـ س ham ہم ہـ م
das دس د س <u>kh</u>at خط خـ ط	

Translation :— kab, jab, rab, das, nal, gaz, <u>kh</u>at, tal.

Exercise 1(b)

sabaq سبق سـ بـ ق safar سفر سـ فـ ر	qadam قدم قـ د م qalam قلم قـ لـ م
namak نمک نـ مـ ک qasam قسم قـ سـ م	

Translation :— qadam, sabad, namak, qasam, Chaman latak, nazar, rabar

Exercise 1(c)

batan بٹن بـ ٹـ ن badan بدن بـ د ن	madad مدد مـ د د kān کان کـ ا ن
kamar کمر کـ مـ ر chār چار چـ ا ر	

Translation :— sāt, tāj, chār, madad, kamar, kān, pān, mān, nām.

PRONOUNCIATION

1. ا alif at the commencement of a word is a mere prop for the letter hamza and has no sound of itself.

2. ت and د (te and dal) are softer and more dental than their English equivalents "T" and "D", the tip of the tongue should touch the upper front teeth when these letters are pronounced.

3. ر re is pronounced distinctly like the French "r".

4. ڑ Re has a heavy sound and when pronouncing it, the tip of the tongue must be turned much farther back.

5. ث s, س s, ص s are in Urdu homophones. They are all pronounced like "s' in sit.

6. ج "G", is always pronounced as "g" in "germ" and never as "g" in "game".

7. چ "Ch" is pronounced as "ch" in "church" and not as "ch" in "chorus".

8. ح h is often pronounced like "h" but should be more guttural than the "h" in huge.

9. ذ z, ز z, ض z, ظ z are in Urdu homophones and are pronounced like the "z" in zeal.

10. ع (') is a strong guttural (consonant).

11. غ gh is a guttural "g" accompanied by a rattling. The "r" in the French grasseye is an approximation only.

12. ق q is a strong guttural, like the "ck" in stuck when pronounced in the throat.

13. ہ "h" as in hand.

PRONUNCIATION OF VOWELS

"a"	is	pronounced	as	"a"	in	Mental
"ā"	"	"	"	"a"	"	Part
"ai"	"	"	"	"a"	"	Bank
"au"	"	"	"	"au"	"	Paul
"ē"	"	"	"	"e"	"	Prey
"i"	"	"	"	"i"	"	Pit
"ī"	"	"	"	"i"	"	Fatigue
"o"	"	"	"	"o"	"	Home
"u"	"	"	"	"u"	"	Put
"ū"	"	"	"	"u"	"	June

SHORT VOWELS

There are three short vowels : Zabar (ـَـ) Zer ( ) and Pesh (ـُـ) which in English are represented by a short "a", short "i" and short "u" respectively. **In practice thney are seldom written or printed.**

1. Zabar — To express the short "a" zabar is used over a letter as ba, بَ na, نَ par پَر and is pronounced like the "u" in the English word "gun".

moment	pal	پَل	پل	grief	gham	غَم	غم
all	sab	سَب	سب	armpit	baghal	بَغَل	بغل
eye-brow	palak	پَلَک	پلک				

2. Zer. — The short "i" is expressed by using zer under a letter, khi خِ as li لِ It is pronounced as "i" in "fin".

heart	dil	دل	دل	pin	pin	پن	پن
day	din	دن	دن	what	kia	کیا	کیا
book	kitab	کتاب	کتاب				

3. Pesh. Similarly, the short "u" is expressed by putting a pesh over a letter, as mu, ju, and is pronounced like the "u" in "put".

bridge	pul	پُل	پُل	you	tum	تُم	تُم
God	Khuda	خدا	خدا	Sun	sūraj	سورج	سورج
bad	bura	بُرا	بُرا				

Exercise II

Translation : pal, ghap, gham, hal, samar, badan kān, sāg, bāgh, chāl, jo, so gir, sir Khuda, kitāb, kiā, turm, din, dil, sāt, nāch, shān.

LONG WOVELS

1. Alif ا Wao و and Ye ی are used in urdu as long vowels.

2. Wao و gives the sound of 'w au, u, and o, whereas ye ی stands for y, ai, i, and e.

3. When و and ی are used at the beginning of a word or syllable it gives the sound of w' and y' as

wahshat وحشت yaklakht یکلخت

Example

Initial	Medial	Final
ا o, as اُوس os	و o, as, موٹا	motā لو lo
اَو au, as, اور aur	و au, as, فَوج	fauj, جَو jau
اُو ū, as, اُون un	و u, as, خُوب	khūb, چاقُو chāqū
اے e, as, ایلچی Elchi	یـ e, as, مین	mēn ے e, as, barē
اَی ai, as, ایسا aisā	یـ ai, as, مَیں	maiṅ ے ai, as,hai
ای ī, as, ایجاد ījad	یـ ī as, یقین	yaqīn ی ī, as, larkī,

Exercise

Read and copy the following:—

حَوض ۔ فَوج ۔ کَون ۔ چَوک ۔ اَور ۔ خَوف ۔ پَیر ۔ سَیر ۔ بَیل ۔ لے ۔

نے ۔ خَیر ۔ بَیر ۔ ایک ۔ جیب ۔ دیگ ۔ دیر ۔ بیر ۔ سیب ۔

شیر ۔ بول ۔ توپ ۔ ڈول ۔ مور ۔ شور ۔ اوس ۔ سوچ ۔

سُورج ۔ چُوڑی ۔ مُولی ۔ آلو ۔ بابُو ۔ چاقُو ۔ خالُو ۔ جُوتا ۔

چُونا ۔ مُورَت ۔ صُورَت ۔

Translation: Hauz, fauz, mauj, kaun, chauk, aur, khauf, pair, sair, bail, ley, ney, khair, bair, ēk, jēb, dēg, dēr, bēr, sēb, shēr, bol, top, dol, mor, shor, os, soch, sūraj, chūrī, mūlī, ālū, bābū, chāqū, khālū, jūtā, chūnā, mūrat, sūrat.

MADD. (ٓ)

The sign of madd, if used over alif ا expresses long "a" in the beginning of a word, as آج

Exercise

Read and write the following:—

آن ۔ آس ۔ آب ۔ آج ۔ آٹا ۔ آغا ۔ آقا ۔ آنا ۔ آگ ۔ آم ۔

آج آپ کیا کر رہے ہیں ۔ جب تک سانس تب تک آس ۔ آٹا نہیں ہے ۔

آرا کہاں ہے ۔ آگ جل رہی ہے ۔ یہ آم خراب ہے ۔ آدمی

بازار میں ہے ۔

Translation: — ām, ānā, āg, āqā, āp, ān, ās, āj, āra, ātā, ālū.

Tashdid (ّ)

Instead of doubling any letter put tashdid on it, as ابّا ab-bā, امّاں am-mān. but in the case of verbs the 'n' is repeated as, مانّنا mān-na,

جانّنا jan-nā.

Exercise

بِلّا ۔ کُتّا ۔ گنّا ۔ چَپّو ۔ چُلّو ۔ بَتّی ۔ سَچّی ۔ حَمّام ۔ حَجّام

کُتّا حَمّام میں چلا گیا ۔ حَجّام نے اسے مارا ۔ موٹا بِلّا بازار

میں ہے ۔ چَپّو کشتی میں ہے ۔ لڑکی سَچّی ہے ۔ بَتّی اُونچی کرو ۔

چُلّو میں پانی دے ۔

Translation : haj-jām, bil-lī, ul-lū, bil-lā, kut-tā, bat-tī, sach-chī, chap-pu.

JAZM (AMPUTATION)

There must always be a woven between two consonants. If there is no sign of zer or pesh, they should be read with zabar (short a), as گَرْم garm, سَرْد sard.

But if this jazm is placed over the middle of two consonants it indicates that here is no short vovel, but that consonants are sounded, as عِلْم ilm, جِسْم jism.

Exercise

Read and copy of the following :—

مُرْغ ۔ فَرْش ۔ شَمْع ۔ کِرچ ۔ مِرچ ۔ عِلْم ۔ جِسْم ۔ گَرْم ۔ سَبْز ۔ سَرْد ۔ سُرْخ ۔

سُرْخ مِرچ تیز ہوتی ہے ۔ موسم سَرْد ہے ۔ فَرْش گیلا ہے ۔ شَمْع خاموش ہے ۔ عِلْم

بڑی دولت ہے ۔ اُس کا جِسْم گَرْم ہے ۔ سِپاہی کے پاس تلوار ہے ۔

Translation : farsh, shama, garm, sabz, sard. sūrkh, ilm, mirch, jism.

HAMZA (HYPEN)

1. Hamza is in Urdu generally the equivalent of a hyphen, as : Fā-eda فائدہ benefit; jā-o جاؤ go. When in a word, one syllable ends in a vowel and the next begins with one, the mark ء is placed over the second vowel to express short a, e, i, o, u, as, پاؤں pā-oṅ, جاؤں jā-ūṅ.

2. If three vowels are used together, the middle vowel is replaced by hamza and takes a loop in the word, as, گائے gā-ē, rū-ī, maka-ī. مکئی روئی

3. Even when one of the vowels is short, hamza is used, as, gayī, گئی kayī. کئی

Exercise

سُوئی ۔ کوئی ۔ کئی ۔ گئی ۔ آؤ ۔ جاؤ ۔ چباؤ ۔ سُناؤ ۔ دیے ۔ لیے ۔

چائے ۔ گائے ۔ دائیں ۔ بائیں ۔

Transliteration:— gāē, chāē, tāsīr, fāeda, kayī, gayī, judāī, gūnjāish.

TANWIN (ADVERBIAL N)

The sign over ا (alif) expresses the adverbial 'n' as, مثلاً maslan, حکماً hukman, etc.

مثلاً ۔ ارادتاً ۔ فوراً ۔ اتفاقاً ۔ قریباً ۔ حکماً ۔

Exercise

Transliteration:— qariban, ittefaqan, fauran, irādatan, maslan, hukman.

ہ (HE)

There are two forms of ہ (he): (i) Butterfly h and (ii) the looped h

(b) The butterfuly h ھ is used either in the beginning or in the middle of a word, but looped h ہ is only used before a vowel, as, پہاڑ

(c) When no vowel sound intervenes between the h and the consonant preceeding it, the butterfuly h ھ is used. Letters coupled with the butterfuly h are called aspirated compounds.

Note the following :— گھر ghar, کھڑکی khirkī, بھالو bhālū, جھم jham, چھوکرا chhokrā, پھل phal, etc.

(d) ہ When it comes at the end of a word and is immediately preceded by zabar (short a), it is silent and is streated as a short a. as, تماشہ tamasha, مردہ murda.

(e) Bothe the medial and final forms are used if an h, is expressed at the end of a word, as, ہاتھ hath, کچھ kuchh.

Note :— A looped h ہ sometimes tames another loop under it, as, ہونا hona, پہنچنا pahunchna.

ں (NASAL ں NUN)

When it comes after a long vowel, the has (ں) a nasal sound. At the end of a word, however, it is written without a dot, as گھاس ghāṅs, مُرغیاں murghīāṅ, māṅ. ماں

Exercise

پانچ ۔ کانچ ۔ رنگ ۔ جنگ ۔ ماں ۔ ہاں ۔ کہاں ۔ یہاں ۔ میں ۔ ہیں ۔
بیں ۔ مُنہہ ۔ سانپ ۔ دانت ۔
جنگ کا کیا رنگ ہے؟ ماں کے ہاں کون ہے؟ کہاں ہیں وہاں گیا
تھا ۔ میرا بھائی کہاں ہے؟ آج یہاں گرمی ہے ۔ میں پہاڑ
پر جاؤں گا ۔ سانپ کے دانت نہیں ہیں ۔ اُس کا مُنہہ بہت چھوٹا
ہے ۔ آج مینہہ برس رہا ہے ۔

Transliteration:— dāṅt, sāṅp, pāṅch, kāṅch, raṅg, jaṅg, māṅ, hāṅ, kāhāṅ, yāhāṅ, mūṅh, mēṅh.

ASPIRATED CONSONENTS

بھ bh	as, بھالو bhalu		دھ dh	as, دھم dham
پھ ph	as, پھول phul		ڈھ dh	as, ڈھال dhal
تھ th	as, تھال thal		ڑھ rh	as گڑھ garh
ٹھ th	as, ٹھیلا thela		کھ kh	as, کھانا khana
جھ jh	as, جھول jhol		گھ gh	as, گھر ghar
چھ chh	as, چھری churi		لھ lh	as, دولھا dulha

Exercise

Read and copy the following:—

بُھوک ۔ پَھل ۔ پُھول ۔ چَھڑی ۔ جھاڑو ۔ تھیلا ۔ ٹھیلا ۔
مَکئی کا بُھٹّا ۔ ریل کا ٹھیلا ۔ زَہرہ کا بھائی ۔ رَتن کی جھاڑو ۔ مَداری کا تھیلا ۔
گُلاب کا پُھول ۔ زُور کی بُھوک ۔ اِحمد کا جُھولا ۔ ابّا کی چَھڑی ۔ آم کا پَھل ۔
اَمجد کی چَھتری ۔ آپا کا جُھومر ۔ چُولھے کی دیگچی ۔

Revisional Exercise :—

دَس تک گِنو ۔ آج کیا دن ہے ؟ گِلاس دے آؤ ۔ لڑکی پانی لائی ۔ کل عید ہے ۔
یہ نیم کا پیڑ ہے ۔ ریل چَلتی ہے ۔ بادل گرجتا ہے ۔ بجلی چمکتی ہے ۔ مُور ناچتا ہے ۔
مُوتی آیا ۔ طوطا بُولتا ہے ۔ شُور نہ کیجیے ۔ بُلبُل کا نغمہ سنیے ۔

ہُدہُد اُڑ گیا ۔ اُستاد کا ادب کرو ۔ خُدا سے دُعا کرو ۔ یہ ایک
مُورت ہے ۔ کیسی خوب صُورت ہے ۔ وہ سُورج نِکلا ۔ ریل آتی ہے ۔
سانپ کا تماشہ ہو رہا ہے ۔ دانت صاف کرو ۔ مینہ خُوب برسا ۔ حوض کا پانی
صاف ہے ۔ وہ انگور کی بیل ہے ۔ یہ گُلاب کا پودا ہے ۔ شمع روشن
کرو ۔ پانی گرم ہے ۔ کشتی چپّو سے چلتی ہے ۔ چُلّو میں پانی لو ۔ حجّام سے
بال کٹوالو ۔

THE NUMERALS

۱	۲	۳	۴	۵	۶	۷	۸	۹	۱۰
1	2	3	4	5	6	7	8	9	10

PART II

THE ARTICLE

"A", "an", and "the" are called the Articles. "A" and "an" are generally translated by "ek" (meaning one), while "the" is omitted in Urdu. Sometimes "the" is translated by Yeh == this and Woh == that, when great precision is required.

Nouns

MASCULINES

Man	Ādmī	آدمی	Paper	Kāghaz	کاغذ
House	Ghar	گھر	Knife	Chāqū	چاقو
Name	Nām	نام	Office	Daftar	دفتر
Water	Pānī	پانی	Servant	Naukar	نوکر
Box	Sandūq	صندوق	Verandah	Barāmda	برآمدہ

FEMININES

Women	Aurat	عورت	Table	Mēz	میز
Hat	Topī	ٹوپی	Book	Kitāb	کتاب
Shop	Dukān	دُکان	Letter	Chitthī	چٹھی
Belt	Pētī	پیٹی	Letter	khat*	خط
Knife	Chhurī	چھری	Stick	Lakrī	لکڑی
Chair	Kursī	کرسی	* Khat	is masculine.	

Preposition

A Preposition is a word that governs a Noun or a Prnoun. The little words "on, to, from, in, of" etc./ are called the Prepositions in English, because they come before the Noun they govern, but their equivalents are called the Post-positions in Urdu because they come after the Noun they govern, thus:—

To	Ko	کو	From	Se	سے
On	Par	پر	In	Men	میں

Examples

To the servant	Servant to	Naukar ko	نوکر کو
From the shop	Shop from	Dukan se	دکان سے
On the table	Table on	Mez par	میز پر
In the box	Box in	Sanduq men	صندوق میں

EXERCISE I(A)

(Translate into English)

Kitāb par. Ādmī sē. Pānī mēṅ. Dukān ko. Chitthi mēṅ. Topī par. Daftar ko. Sandūq sē. Aurat ko. Ghar mēṅ. Kāghaz par. naukar sē. Pētī mēṅ. Chhurī se.

EXERCISE 1(B)

(Translate into Urdu)

To the woman. In the house. On the paper. From the servant. On the water. In the letter. To the office. On the box. From the man. In the belt. To the shop.

Verbs

Is	Hai	ہے	Go	Jāo	جاؤ
Come	Āo	آؤ	Bring	Lāo	لاؤ
Wait	Thairo	ٹھہرو	Send	Bhējo	بھیجو
Take away	Lējāo		Take to	Lējāo	لے جاؤ

It must be remembered that in Urdu the position of the Verb is at the extreme end of the sentence. The following examples should be read carefully, and the learner should try to notice and remember the arrangement of words in them.

Examples

1. Go to the office (Office, to go)— Daftar ko jāo
2. Come in the shop (Shop in, come) Dukan mēn̆ āo.
3. Wait in the house (House in, wait) — Ghar mēn̆ thairo.
4. The book is on the table (Book, table on, is) —Kitāb mēz par hai.
5. The letter is in the box (Letter, box in, is) — Chitthi sanduq men hai.
6. Bring the hat from the shop (Hat, shop from, bring) — Topī dukān sē lao.
7. Put the book in the box (Book, box in, put) — Kitāb sandūq mēn̆ rakho.
8. Take this letter to the office (This letter, office to, take away)— Yeh chitthī daftar ko lējāo.

EXERCISE 2(A)

(Translate into English)

Daftār ko āo. Ghar mēn̆ thairo. Dukān ko jāo. Chitthī sandūq mēn̆ hai. Topī mēz par hai. Mēz daftar sē lāo. Woh kāghaz sandūq mēn̆ rakho. Yeh sandūq ghar mēn̆ rakho.

EXERCISE 2(B)

(Translate into Urdu)

Come in the house. Go to the shop. Wait in the office. The hat is in the box. The letter is on the table. The table is in the shop. Bring the box to the shop. Put the paper in the book. Take (away) this book to the office. Send the hat to the house. Bring the stick from the house. Put the knife on the table. Wait on the verandah.

Interrogatives

Who	Kaun	کون	Whose	Kiskā	کس کا
Which	Kaunsā	کونسا	How far	Kitni dūr	کتنی دور
Why	Kīon̆	کیوں	What	Kīā	کیا
Where	Kahān̆	کہاں	When	Kab	کب

It will be noticed that in English sometimes an Interrogative is used before a Verb; as "Who is that man?" and sometimes it is used before a Noun; as, "Whose house is that?" The same idea must be observed in urdu Sentenses.

Note :— Never start an Urdu sentence with an Interrogative.

The answer to an Interrogative sentence in Urdu must start with the same word as the qeustion did as,

Question :— Mez par kia hai? Answer :— Mez per kitab hai

Question :— Kitab kahan hai? Answer :— Kitab Mez par hai.

EXAMPLES

1.	Who is that man? (that man **who** is)	—	Woh ādmī kaun hai?
2.	Whose house is that? (that **whose** house is)	—	Woh kiskā ghar hai.
3.	What is on the table? (table on, **what** is)	—	Mēz par kīā hail?
4.	Whose servant is in the house? (house in **whose** servant is)	—	Ghar mēn̈ kiskā naukar hai?
5.	Where is the servant? (Servant, **where** is)	—	Naukar kahān̈ hai?

EXERCISE 3(A)

(Translate into English)

Woh kaun hai? Yeh kiskā ghar hai? Daftar mēn̈ kaun hai? Topī kahān̈ hai? Woh kiskā naukar hai? Yeh kīā kitāb hai? Pētī sandūq mēn̈ kīon̈ hai? Woh kaunsā kāg͟haz hai? Woh kaun ādmī hai? Chitthī kahān̈ hai? Woh kaunsā ghar hai? Daftar kahān̈ hai?

EXERCISE 3(B)

(Translate into Urdu)

Whose paper is that? What is in the book? Where is the hat? What book is that? Who is in the shop. The servant is in the shop. Whose servant? Why is the man here? What is on the table? Which knife is that? Why is the woman in the office?

Possessive Pronouns

My	Mērā	میرا	Our	Hamārā	ہمارا
Your	Tumhārā	تمہارا	His or Her	Uskā (ooska)	اُسکا

Adverbs

Here	Yahāň	یہاں	There	Wahāň	وہاں
O'clock	Baje	بجے	And (*Conj.*)	Aur	اور
Yes	Jī Hāň	جی ہاں	No	Jī Nahiň	جی نہیں
Don't	Mat	مت	Now	Ab	اب

Observation

Possessive pronouns have the same position in Urdu as they have in English i.e., they must precede the Noun they govern.

EXAMPLES

1. What is your name? (Your name, what, is) — Tumhārā nām kīā hai?
2. My servant is in the house (My servant, house in, is) — Mērā naukar ghar mēň hai).
3. Where is his house? (His house, where, is) — Uskā ghar kahāň hai?
4. Your knife is on the table (Your knife, table on, is) — Tumhārā chāqū mēz par hai.

Note :— The Adverb must be used just before the Verb: as,

1. Bring that table here (That table, ***here*** bring) — Woh mēz yahāň lāo.
2. Put this letter there (This letter, ***there*** put) — Yeh chitthī wāhāň rakho.
3. Come here at two o'clock (Two o'clock, ***here*** come) — Do bajē yāhāň āo.
4. The servant is not in the house (Servant, house in, not is) — Naukar ghar men nahīň hai.

EXERCISE 4(A)

(Translate into English)

Tumhārā nām kīā hai? Mērā nam Abdul hai. Uskā ghar kahāň hai? Uskā ghar bāzār mēň hai. Woh mēz yahāň lāo. Mērī topī mēz per rakho. Woh ādmī ghar mēň nahiň hai. Daftar ko mat jāo. Pānī mēz par nahiň hai. Mera kāghaz daftar ko lējāo. Pānī mēz par mat rakho. Hamārā naukar daftar mēň hai.

EXERCISE 4(B)

(Translate into Urdu)

Where is my servant? Your servant is in the house. Where is his box? His box is in the office. Go there at one o'clock. Bring my hat from the office. His servant is not in the office. Don't go to the house. Don't bring the box here. Send my box to the office. The hat is not on the table. Don't put the box on the table.

Pronouns

I	Maiň	میں	He, She	Woh	وہ
We	Ham	ہم	Thou	Tū	تو
You	Tum	تم	They	Woh	وہ
Am	Hūň	ہوں	Is	Hai	ہے
Art (thou)	Hai	ہے	Are (you)	Ho	ہو
Are	Haiň	ہیں			
I am	Main hūň	میں ہوں	He is, She is	Woh hai	وہ ہے
We are	Ham haiň	ہم ہیں	Thou are	Tu hai	تو ہے
You are	Tum ho	تم ہو	They are	Woh haiň	وہ ہیں

(i) 'Tum' is used for 'you' singular and plural, just as in English. It is plural in form though it may be singular or plural in use. The real second person singular 'tu' is seldom used.

(ii) 'Tum'. (you) is only used to inferiors. To equals or superiors always use 'āp' with the third person plural verb (i.e. the form used with 'woh they). Āpkā—your.

Note the use and position of the above in the following examples.

EXAMPLES

1. I am his servant (I, his servant, am) — Maiň, uskā naukar, hūň.

2. He is in the house (He, house in, is) — Woh, ghar mēň, hai.

3. Who are you? (you, who, are) — Tum kaun ho? (Polite) Āp kaun haiň.

4. We are in the office (We, office in, are) — Ham, daftar mēň, haiň.

5. You are in the shop (You, shop in, are) — Tum, dukān mēň, ho, or, Āp dukān mēň, haiň.

6. They are not in the shop (They, shop in, not are) — Woh, dukān mēň, nahīň haiň.

7. I am not your servant (I, your servant, not am) — Maiň, tumhārā naukar, nahiň hūň. (or) Maiň āpkā naukar nahiň hūň.

EXERCISE 5(A)

(Translate into English)

Tum kaun ho? Maiṅ āpkā naukar hūṅ. Tumhārā ghar kahāṅ hai? Mērā ghar Delhi mēṅ hai. Woh daftar mēṅ hai. Ham dukān mēṅ haiṅ. Āpkā naukar ghar mēṅ hai. Woh daftar mēṅ nahiṅ hai. Woh mērā naukar hai. Tum kahāṅ ho? Maiṅ ghar mēṅ hūṅ. Tum daftar mēṅ nahiṅ ho. Uskā ghar bāzāār mēṅ nahiṅ hai.

Exercise 5(b)

(Translate into Urdu)

Who is he? He is my servant. I am in the office. They are not men. Where are you? He is in the office. We are in the shop. I am a dhobi. Where is your house? He is not here. I am not his servant. They are not in the shop. He is not in my office. Which is your box.

Revisional Exercise 6(a)

1. Take this box to the shop and put it on the table. 2 Why is my servant not in the house? 3. What is your name, where is your house and why are you here? 4. Don't bring my box to the office now. 5. How far is your house from the shop? 6. The book is in the box and the box is in the house. 7. He is not here.

Revisional Exercise 6(b)

۱۔ دفتر کو آؤ۔ ۲۔ میرا خط میز پر رکھو۔ ۳۔ یہ صندوق گھر کو لے جاؤ۔ ۴۔ وہ کون ہے؟ ۵۔ ٹوپی کہاں ہے؟ ۶۔ وہ کس کا نوکر ہے؟۔ ۷۔ یہ کیا کتاب ہے؟ ۸۔ پیٹی صندوق میں کیوں ہے؟ ۹۔ وہ کونسا کاغذ ہے؟ ۱۰۔ یہ تمہاری چٹھی نہیں ہے؟ ۱۱۔ احمد کہاں ہے؟ ۱۲۔ پانی میز پر مت رکھو۔ ۱۳۔ تمہارا نام کیا ہے؟ ۱۴۔ میرا نام عبدل ہے۔ ۱۵۔ بازار کو مت جاؤ۔ ۱۶۔ وہ میز یہاں لاؤ۔ ۱۷۔ میری کتاب دفتر کو بھیجو۔ ۱۸۔ یہ صندوق دفتر کو لے جاؤ اور میز پر رکھو۔ ۱۹۔ میرا نوکر گھر میں کیوں نہیں ہے؟ ۲۰۔ تمہارا نام کیا ہے، تمہارا گھر کہاں ہے اور تم یہاں کیوں ہو؟ ۲۱۔ میرا صندوق دفتر کو اب مت لاؤ۔ ۲۲۔ آپ کا گھر دفتر سے کتنی دور ہے؟ ۲۳۔ میرا گھر دفتر سے پانچ میل دور ہے۔ ۲۴۔ کتاب صندوق میں ہے اور صندوق دکان میں ہے۔

PART III

THE NOUN

The name of a person, place or thing is called a Noun; as James, Bombay, chair, etc.

NOUNS

Masculines

Boy	Laṙkā	لڑکا	Son	Bēṭā	بیٹا
Horse	Ghoṙā	گھوڑا	Dog	Kuttā	کتّا
Room	Kamra	کمرہ	Door	Darwāza	دروازہ
Cloth	Kapṙā	کپڑا	Egg	Anḍā	انڈا
Envelope	Lifāfa	لفافہ	Lock	Tālā	تالا
Hour, Clock	Ghanta	گھنٹہ	Bathroom	Ghusl Khāna	غسلخانہ
Brother	Bhāī	بھائی	Husband	Khāwind	خاوند

Feminines

Girl	Laṙkī	لڑکی	Daughter	Bēṭī	بیٹی
Mare	Ghoṙī	گھوڑی	Bitch	Kutyā	کتیا
Window	Khiṙkī	کھڑکی	Key	Chābī	چابی
Watch	Ghaṙī	گھڑی	Carriage	Gāṙī	گاڑی
Turban	Pagṙī	پگڑی	Ink	Siāhī	سیاہی
Saddle	Zīn	زین	Inkpot	Dawāt	دوات
Sister	Bahen	بہن	Wife	Bīwī	بیوی

Gender

2. The Urdu language has only two Genders, i.e., the Masculine Gender and the Feminine Gender, and no Neuter Gender.

Males are called Masculine and Females Feminine.

(a) Nouns that end in "a", with very few exceptions, are Masculines : as, Larkā—a boy; Kaprā—cloth.

(b) Nouns that end in "i" are almost always Feminine: as, Larkī—a girl; Gārī—a carriage. Ādmī (man) or bhāī (brother) are masculines by meaning.

The Gender of inanimate Nouns that do not end in "a" or "i" must be learnt by practice.

Number

3. There are two Numbers, i.e., the Singular and the Plural. One thing is called Singular, and more than one, Plural. The rules forming the Plurals are quite simple.

The following are the four rules for forming the Nominative Plurals.

Masculine

1. If a Masculine Noun ends in "a" change the "a" into "e"; as, Lark ā — one boy; Larkē—boys.
2. If a Masculine Noun does not end in "a" it remains unaltered; as Ghar— one house; Chār ghar—four houses.

Feminine

1. If a Feminine Noun ends in "i" add " āň" as, Larkī—a girl; Larkīāň—girls.
2. If a Feminine Noun does not end in "i" add " ēň"; as, Kitāb—a book; Kitābēň—books.

EXERCISE 7

Form the Nominative Plurals of

Masculine Nouns :—

Bētā, Ghoṛā, Daftar, Tālā, Chāqū, Naukar, Lifāfa, Bhāī, Kamra, Kuttā, Ghanta, Larkā, Andā, Nām, Darwāza, Sandūq, Barāmda, Ghar.

Feminine Nouns :—

Chābi, Pētī, Mēz, Gāṛī, Dawāt, Lakṛī, Dukān, Aurat, Chiṭṭhī, Topī, Zīn, Bīwī, Kitāb, Khiṛkī, Pagṛī, Gharī.

The Cases

4. The most important are the Nominative and the Objective cases.

(a) A Noun is said to be in the Nominative Case, when it is the name of something talked about, and when it is not governed by any Preposition; as, "The soldier drills". Here the "soldier" is in the Nominative Case because he does something.

(b) A Noun is said to be in the Objective Case, when something is done to it, or when it is governed by a Preposition or a Transitive Verb; as, "He sees the horse", "He was on the horse." In both sentences "horse" is in the Objective Case.

(c) In English no alteration is made in the actual spelling of a Noun when it is Objective, but in Urdu alterations, in accordance with Rules given hereafter, are made in certain cases where the objective is governed by a Post-Position. All cases, except the Nominative Case, are called the Oblique Cases, which have different names according to the Post-Position following them.

Thus a Noun is said to be in the

Genitive	Case if	followed	by	"kā"— of
Dative	"	"	"	ko — to
Locative	"	"	"	par or mēn̆—at
Ablative	"	"	"	sē—with
Agent	"	"	"	nē—by
Vocative	"	"	"	ai or o—O!

In the Accusative case the Noun is not govered by any Post-Position, because it is governed by a Transitive Verb; as, kill a dog—ēk kutta maro.

Note :— A Noun in the Accusative case has either the same form as a Nominative, as in English, or is expressed by "ko", like the Dative.

Oblique Singular

(Singular Nouns followed by Post-Positions)

1. Masculine Singular Nouns ending in "a" change the "a" into "e" before a Post-Position for the sake of euphony; as,

   On the horse, Ghoṙē par گھوڑے پر (not Ghoṙa par).

   In the room, Kamrē mēn̆ کمرے میں (not Kamra mēn̆).

2. Masculine Singular Nouns not ending in "a" do not change.
3. Feminine Singular Nouns never change.

OBLIQUE PLURALS

The Oblique Plurals have but one rule, which is that all Plural Nouns (of whatever Gender or ending) have the suffix "on" when followed by a Post-Position. If, however, a Masculine Singular Noun ends in "a" the "a" is dropped before "on" for the sake of euphony; as :—

Man	ādmī	—	To the men	ādmīoṅ ko	آدمیوں کو
Table	mēz	—	On the tables	mēzoṅ par	میزوں پر
House	ghar	—	In the houses	gharoṅ mēṅ	گھروں میں
Office	daftar	—	From the offices	daftaroṅ sē	دفتروں سے
Dog	kuttā	—	To the dogs	kūttoṅ ko	کتّوں کو
Cloth	kāpṛā	—	On the clothes	kapṛoṅ par	کپڑوں پر

EXERCISE 8(A)

(On the Oblique Singular and Plural)

Translate into English:—

Sandūq mēṅ	صندوق میں	Sandūqoṅ mēṅ	صندوقوں میں
Ghar mēṅ	گھر میں	Gharoṅ mēṅ	گھروں میں
Laṛkē ko	لڑکے کو	Laṛkoṅ ko	لڑکوں کو
Ghoṛē sē	گھوڑے سے	Ghoṛoṅ sē	گھوڑوں سے
Lifāfē mēṅ	لفافے میں	Lifāfoṅ mēṅ	لفافوں میں
Ghoṛī par	گھوڑی پر	Ghoṛīoṅ par	گھوڑیوں پر
Pēṭī mēṅ	پیٹی میں	Pēṭīoṅ mēṅ	پیٹیوں میں
Naukar ko	نوکر کو	Naukaroṅ ko	نوکروں کو

EXERCISE 8(B)

Translate into Urdu:—

From the office	From the offices	In the window	In the windows
In the inkpot	In the inkpots	From the door	From the doors
To the mare	To the mares	On the horse	On the horses
To the dog	To the dogs	In the house	In the houses
In the box	In the boxes		

Revisional Exercise 9

Two Masculine Nouns are declined on page 30 one of them ending in "a" and the other not ending in "a".

Two Feminine Nouns are declined on page 30, one ending in "i" and the other not ending in "i".

Decline all the Nouns given under them according to the model.

MASCULINES

Singular			Plural	
Nominative		Oblique	Nominative	Oblique
گھوڑا	Ghoṛa	Ghoṛe ko گھوڑے کو	Ghoṛe گھوڑے	Ghoṛon ko گھوڑوں کو
دفتر	Daftar			Daftaron ko دفتروں کو
چاقو	Chaqu			
نوکر	Naukar			
لفافہ	Lifafa			
بھائی	Bhāi			
کمرہ	Kamra			
کُتّا	Kuttā			
گھنٹہ	Ghanta			
لڑکا	Larkā			
انڈا	Andā			
نام	Nām			
دروازہ	Darwāza			
صندوق	Sandūq			
برآمدہ	Barāmda			
گھر	Ghar			

Note :* — *Put a dash where a Noun undergoes no change.

FEMININES

Singular			Plural	
Nominative		Oblique	Nominative	Oblique
لڑکی	Laṙkī	Laṙkī ko لڑکی کو	Laṙkīāṅ لڑکیاں	Laṙkīoṅ ko لڑکیوں کو
عورت	Aurat	—	Auratēṅ عورتیں	Auratoṅ ko عورتوں کو
میز	Mēz			
گاڑی	Gāṙī			
دوات	Dawāt			
چھری	Chhurī			
دوکان	Dukān			
چٹھی	Chiṭṭhī			
ٹوپی	Ṭopī			
زین	Zīn			
بیوی	Bīwī			
کتاب	Kitāb			
کھڑکی	Khiṙkī			
پگڑی	Pagṙī			
بہن	Bahen			
گھڑی	Ghaṙī			

Note :— Put a dash where a Noun undergoes no change.

Past Auxiliary Verbs

Singular		Plural	
Was (Masc.)—thā	تھا	Were (Masc.) thē	تھے
Was (Fem.)—thī	تھی	Were (Fem.)—thīṅ	تھیں

EXAMPLES

1. The boy was in the house (boy, house in, was) —
   Laṙkā ghar mēṅ thā. لڑکا گھر میں تھا
2. The man was on the horse (man, horse on, was)—
   Ādmī ghoṙē par thā. آدمی گھوڑے پر تھا
3. The girl was in the room (girl, room in, was)—
   Laṙkī kamrē mēṅ thī لڑکی کمرے میں تھی
4. The books were on the tables (books, tables on, were—
   Kitābēṅ mēzoṅ par thīṅ. کتابیں میزوں پر تھیں
5. The boys were in the offices (boys, offices in, were) —
   Laṙkē daftaroṅ mēṅ thē.. لڑکے دفتروں میں تھے

Exercise 10(a)

1. Laṙkā ghoṙē par thā. 2. Laṙkē ghoṙoṅ par thē. 3. Kamrē mēṅ ēk darwāza thā. 4. Kamroṅ mēṅ chār darwāzē the. 5. Ghanṭa daftar mēṅ thā. 6. Ghanṭē daftaroṅ mēṅ thē. 7. Laṙkī kamrē mēṅ thī. 8. Laṙkīāṅ kamroṅ mēṅ thīṅ. 9. Aurat gāṙī mēṅ thī. 10. Auratēṅ gāṙī mēṅ thīṅ. 11. Kitāb sandūq mēṅ thī. 12. Kitābēṅ sandūqoṅ mēṅ thīṅ. 13. Naukar barāmdē mēṅ thā. 14. Naukar barāmdoṅ mēṅ thē. 15. Topī mēz par thī. 16. Topīāṅ mēzoṅ par thīṅ. 17. Chābī tālē mēṅ thī. 18. Chābīāṅ tāloṅ mēṅ thīṅ. 19. Andā dukān mēṅ thā. 20. Andē dukānon mēṅ thē. 21. Dawāt mēz par thī. 22. Dawātēṅ mēzon par thīṅ.

EXERCISE 10(B)

1. The cloth was in the box. 2. The clothes were in the boxes. 3. The son was in the room. 4. The sons were in the rooms. 5. The letter was in the envelope. 6. The letters were in the envclopes. 7. The man was in the carriage. 8. The men were in the carriages. 9. The key was on the table. 10. The keys were on the tables. 11. The boy was on the horse. 12. The boys were on the horses. 13. The dog was on the verandah. 14. The dogs were on the verandahs. 15. The man was in the shop. 16. The men were in the shops. 17. The belt was in the box. 18. The belts were in the boxes. 19. The knife was on the table. 20. The knives were on the tables. 21. The woman was on the horse. 22. The women were on the horses. 23. The boy was on the horse and the girl was on the mare. 24. The boys were on the horses and the girls were on the mares.

PRONOUN

A Pronoun is a word used in place of a Noun, as I, we, you, he, they, she, it, etc.

Declensions of Pronouns

1st Person			
Singular			
Nom.	I	Main	میں
Obique	My	Mera	میرا
	To me	Mujh ko	مجھ کو
	On me	Mujh par	مجھ پر
	In me	Mujh Mēn̆	مجھ میں
	From me	Mujh Sē	مجھ کو

Plural			
	We	Ham	ہم
	Our	Hamārā	ہمارا
	To us	Ham ko	ہم کو
	On us	Ham par	ہم پر
	In us	Ham mēň	ہم میں
	From us	Ham sē	ہم سے

2nd Person			
Singular			
Nom.	Thou	Tū	تو
Obique	Thy	Tērā	تیرا
	To Thee	Tujh ko	تجھ کو
	On "	" par	تجھ پر
	In "	" mēň	تجھ میں
	From "	" sē	تجھ سے
Plural			
	You	Tum/Āp	تم / آپ
	Your	Tumhārā/Āp kā	تمہارا / آپ کا
	To you	Tum ko/Āp ko	تم کو / آپ کو
	On "	" par/Āp par	تم پر / آپ پر
	In "	" mēň /Āp mēň	تم میں / آپ میں
	From "	" sē/Āp sē	تم سے / آپ سے

3rd Person

Singular

Nom.	He	Woh	وہ	His	Us kā	اُس کا
Obique	To him	Us ko	اُس کو	On him	Us par	اُس پر
	In him	Us mēn̆	اُس میں	From him	Us sē	اُس سے

Plural

They	Woh	وہ	Their	Un kā	اُن کا
To them	Un ko	اُن کو	On them	Un par	اُن پر
In them	Un mēn̆	اُن میں	From them	Un sē	اُن سے

Note :— "Woh" means "He, she, it, that, they, and those."

Accusative case

Singular			Plural		
Me	Mujhē	مجھے	Us	Hamēn̆	ہمیں
Thee	Tujhē	تجھے	You	Tumhēn̆	تمہیں
Him or her	Usē	اسے	Them	Unhēn̆	انہیں

DEMONSTRATIVE PRONOUNS

Singular			Plural		
This	Yeh	یہ	These	Yeh	یہ
To this	Is ko	اِس کو	Of these	In kā	اِن کا
Of this	Is kā	اِس کا	On these	In par	اِن پر
From this	Is sē	اِس سے	In these	In mēn̆	اِن میں

REMOTE

Singular			Plural		
That	Woh	وہ	Those	Woh	وہ
Of that	Us kā	اُس کا	Of those	Un kā	اُن کا
To that	Us ko	اُس کو	On those	Un par	اُن پر
From that	Us sē	اُس سے	In those	Un mēñ	اُن میں

Note :— The easiest way to remember the above is that before a Post-position, or before a Noun followed by a Post-position

Yeh	(this)	is changed	into	"is"	اِس
Yeh	(these)	"	"	"in"	اِن
Woh	(that)	"	"	"us"	اُس
Woh	(those)	"	"	"un"	اُن

This horse,	yeh ghořā;	On this horse,	is ghořē par
These horses,	yeh ghořē;	On these horses,	in ghořoñ par
That horse,	woh ghořā;	on that horse,	us ghořē par
Those horses,	woh ghořē;	On those horses,	un ghořoñ par

CONJUGATION OF THE VERB— "HONA" (TO BE)

PRESENT

Singular					
I am	Maiñ hūñ	میں ہوں	Thou art	Tū hai	تو ہے
He or she is	Woh hai	وہ ہے			

Plural					
We are	Ham haiǹ	ہم ہیں	You are	Tum ho	تم ہو
They are	Woh haiǹ	وہ ہیں			
PAST					
Singular					
I was	Maiǹ thā	میں تھا	Thou wast	Tū thā	تو تھا
He was	Woh thā	وہ تھا	She was	Woh thī	وہ تھی
Plural					
We were	Ham thē	ہم تھے	You were	Tum thē	تم تھے
They were	Woh thē	وہ تھے	They were	Woh thīǹ	وہ تھیں
FUTURE					
Singular					
I shall be	Maiǹ hoǹgā	میں ہونگا	Thou wilt be	Tū hogā	تو ہوگا
He will be	Woh hogā	وہ ہوگا	She will be	Woh hogī	وہ ہوگی
Plural					
We will be	Ham hoǹgē	ہم ہونگے	You will be	Tum hogē	تم ہوگے
They will be	Woh hoǹgē	وہ ہونگے	They will be	Woh hoǹgī	وہ ہونگی

EXAMPLES

I am in the room.	Maiǹ kamṙē mēǹ hūǹ.
You are on the horse.	Tum ghoṙē par ho.
He was my son.	Woh mērā bētā thā.
They will be on the horses.	Woh ghoṙoǹ par hoǹge.

EXERCISE 11(A)

1. Maiṅ daftar mēṅ thā. 2. Woh ghoṙī par thī. 3. Woh ghoṙē par thā. 4. Woh mērā bētā hai. 5. Āp kā naukar kamrē mēṅ hai. 6. Tum daftar mēṅ ho. 7. Woh g͟husl k͟hānē mēṅ hai. 8. Maiṅ ghar mēṅ hoṅgā. 9. Woh dukān mēṅ hoṅge. 10. Ham gāṙī mēṅ thē. 11. Maiṅ ghoṙē par hūṅ. 12. Āp gāṙī mēṅ thē 13. Maiṅ uskā naukar hūṅ.

EXERCISE 11(B)

1. I am your servant. 2. He is my brother 3. We are in the office. 4. You are on the horse. 5. They are men. 6. I was in the room. 7. She was on the verandah. 8. They were on the horses. 9. The women were on the mares. 10. I shall be in the house. 11. The letters will be in the boxes. 12. The men will be in the shops. 13. The women will be in the rooms.

THE GENITIVE CASE

(or the Use of "kā, kē, or kī" - of)

In Urdu the order of words connected by "of" is the reverse of that used in English, i.e., the word which is used before "of" in English comes after "kā" in Urdu and vice versa; as,

The door of the house (will become)
House's door — ghar kā darwāza.

The key of the lock of the office (will become)
Office's lock's key—Daftar kē tālē kī chābī.

Note : — It follows that when "s" is used in English, the order of the words does not change. The place of "s" is taken by "kā", 'kē' or 'kī' according to the Gender, Number and Case of the Noun that follows; as,

The man's house or The house of the man	—	man's house, ādmī ka ghar آدمی کا گھر
The woman's son or The son of the woman	—	woman's son, aurat kā bētā. عورت کا بیٹا

The following rules regarding the use of "kā, kē and kī" must be carefully learnt and practised.

1. "Kā" is used before a Masculine Singular Noun, when the latter is not followed by a Post-position; as

The sister's son	Bahen kā bētā	بہن کا بیٹا
The door of the house	Ghar kā darwāza	گھر کا دروازہ

2. "Kē" is used before Masculine Singular Noun, when the latter is followed by a Post-position; as,

To the sister's son	Bahen kē bētē ko	بہن کے بیٹے کو
In the door of the house	Ghar kē darwāzē mēn̆ گھر کے دروازے میں	

3. "Kē" is also used before all Masculine Plural Nouns, whether followed by a Post-position or not; as,

In the door of the house	Ghar kē darwāzē mēn̆
The sister's sons	Bahen kē bētē
To the sister's sons	Bahen kē bēton̆ ko
The doors of the house	Ghar kē darwāzē
In the doors of the house	Ghar kē darwāzon̆ mēn̆

4. "Kī" is used before all Feminine Nouns whether Singular or Plural, or whether followed by a Post-Position or not; as,

The servant's daughter	Naukar kī bētī	نوکر کی بیٹی
To the servant's daughter	Naukar kī bētī ko	نوکر کی بیٹی کو
The servant's daughters	Naukar kī bētīāṅ	نوکر کی بیٹیاں
To the servant's daughters	Naukar kī bētīoṅ ko	نوکر کی بیٹیوں کو

It must be remembered that "kā", being a Post-position inflects the preceding Noun, while itself agrees with the Noun which it precedes; as,

The boy's mare	Laṙkē kī ghoṙī	لڑکے کی گھوڑی
The boys' mares	Laṙkoṅ ki ghoṙīāṅ	لڑکوں کی گھوڑیاں

In the above sentences "kā" has changed "laṙkā" into "laṙkē and laṙkoṅ" respectively while it has itself become "kī" to agree with the following Feminine Noun "ghoṙī".

EXAMPLES

1.	The woman's son is in the office.	Aurat kā bētā daftar mēṅ hai.
2.	The servant's son was on the horse.	Naukar kā bētā ghoṙē par thā.
3.	The boy's clothes are in the box.	Laṙkē kē kaprē sandūq mēṅ haiṅ.
4.	The dog was in the boy's room.	Kuttā laṙkē kē kamrē mēṅ thā.
5.	The girls were on the women's horses.	Laṙkīāṅ auratoṅ kē ghoṙoṅ par thīṅ.
6.	The matting of the room was in the tailor's shop.	Kamrē kī chatāī darzī kī dukān mēṅ thī.

7.	The boys' father was on the horse.	Lařkoň kā bāp ghořē par thā
8.	The mother of the girls is in the room.	Larkīoň kī māň kamrē mēň hai.
9.	The key of thc lock of the office is on the table.	Daftar kē tālē kī chābī mēz par hai.
10.	Your servant's turban was in the box.	Āp kē naukar kī pagřī sandūq mēň thī.

EXERCISE 12(A)

(For new words see over page)

1. Darzī kā bēṭā. 2. Naukar kē kapřē. 3. Dost kī bēṭī. 4. Bēṭī kā dost. 5. Ghorē kī qīmat. 6. Palaňg kī chādar sandūq mēň hai. 7. Lařkē kī kitābēň kamrē kē konē mēň haiň. 8. Naukar kē kapřē dhobī kē ghar mēň haiň. 9. Mēz kē kapřē kī qīmat jēb mēň hai. 10. Is ādmī kī dukān Sadar Bāzār mēň hai. 11. Dost kī bētīāň ghořīoň par thīň. 12. Palaňg ghar kī chhat par hai. 13. Woh chīzēň kamrē kē konē mēň haiň. 14. Bādshāh kī taswīr khazānē kē kamrē kī dīwār par hai. 15. Is ādmī kā dost tār ghar mēň hai. 16. Daftar kē tāloň kī chābīāň Alī Sāheb kē kamrē ko lējāo. 17. Ahmed sāheb kē naukar kē bētē kē sandūq kī chābī sāīs kī jēb mēň thī.

WORDS

Masculines					
Order	Hukm	حکم	Butcher	Qasāī	قصائی
Tailor	Darzī	درزی	Washerman	Dhobī	دھوبی
Tiger	Shēr	شیر	King	Bādshāh	بادشاہ
Beast	Jānwar	جانور	Bed	Palaňg	پلنگ
Bedding	Bistar	بستر	Corner	Kona	کونہ
Telegraph Office	Tār ghar	تار گھر	Friend,	Dost	دوست
Post Office	Dāk khānā	ڈاکخانہ	Treasury	Khazāna	خزانہ
Pen	Qalam	قلم	Father	Bāp	باپ

Feminines					
Pocket	Jēb	جیب	Gun	Bandūq	بندوق
Barrel (gun)	Nālī	نالی	Roof	Chhat	چھت
Sheet	Chādar	چادر	Thing	Chīz	چیز
Washer woman	Dhoban	دھوبن	Wall	Dīwār	دیوار
Picture	Taswīr	تصویر	Price	Qīmat	قیمت
Sunshine	Dhūp	دھوپ	Moonlight	Chāndnī	چاندنی
Cantonment	Chhāonī	چھاونی	Court (Justice)	Adālat	عدالت
Bread	Roṭī	روٹی	Mother	Māň	ماں

1. The man's dog. 2. The son's room. 3. The barrel of the gun. 4. I was on the boy's horse. 5. The husband's clothes were in the box. 6. The washerman's house is in the Sadar Bazar. 7. The woman's book was on the table. 8. This is the Director's order. 9. The horse of the carriage. 10. The boy's carriage. 11. The key of the box was in the pocket. 12. The husbands of the women were on the horses. 13. The daughters of the servants are in the room. 14. The butcher's servant was in the tailor's shop. 15. The tiger is the king of the beasts of the jungle. 16. The sheet of the bed is in the washerman's house.

THE ADJECTIVES

An Adjective is a word joined to a Noun to show its quality (as a strong man); size (as, a large book); colour (as, a red coat) or to describe it in any way.

Adjectives

Read the following words of opposite meaning across the page.

True	Sach-chā	سچّا	False (liar)	Jhutā	جھوٹا
Hot	Garm	گرم	Cold	Thandā	ٹھنڈا
Dry	Sūkhā	سُوکھا	Wet	Gīlā	گیلا
Clean, clear	Sāf	صاف	Dirty	Mailā	میلا
Great, large	Baṙā	بڑا	Small, little	Chhoṭā	چھوٹا
High, Big	Uṅchā	اُونچا	Low	Nīchā	نیچا
Long, tall	Lambā	لمبا	Short	Chhotā	چھوٹا
Wide	Chauṙā	چوڑا	Narrow	Taṅg	تنگ
Deep	Gahrā	گہرا	Shallow	Uthlā	اُتھلا
All	Sab	سب	Few	Chand	چند
Dark	Andhērā	اندھیرا	Bright	Raushan	روشن
Young (youthful)	Jawān	جوان	Old, (animate)	Buddhā	بُڈھا
New	Nayā	نیا	Old (inanimate)	Purānā	پُرانا
Much	Bahut	بہت	A little (quantity)	Thoṙā	تھوڑا
Good	Ach-chhā	اچھا	Bad	Kharāb or Burā	خراب بُرا

The adjectives, as in English, are used immediately before their Nouns. Adjectives that do not end in "a" undergo no change, but those that end in "a" change the "a" into "e" or "i", as the case may be, for Gender, Number and Case.

1. If a Masculine Singular Noun is not followed by a Post-position, the final "a" of the Adjectives does not change; as, a large dog— ēk bařā kūttā.

2. If a Masculine Singular Noun is followed by a Post-position and before all Masculine Plural Nouns (whether followed by a Post-position or not) the final "a" of the Adjective is changed into "e"; as,

To the large dog.	Bařē kuttē ko.	بڑے کُتّے کو
The large dogs.	Bařē kuttē.	بڑے کُتّے
To the large dogs.	Bařē kuttoň ko.	بڑے کُتّوں کو

3. The final "a" of the Adjective is changed into "i" before all Feminine Nouns, whether Singular or Plural or whether followed by a Post-Position or not; as,

A large mare.	Bařī ghořī.	بڑی گھوڑی
On the large mare.	Bařī ghořī par.	بڑی گھوڑی پر
On the large mares.	Bařī ghořīoň par.	بڑی گھوڑیوں پر

Observation : — Adjectives never have the endings "aň", "eň" and "oň". For instance we cannot say — Bařīāň ghořīāň; Bařīoň ghořīoň par (or) Bařoň ghořoň par.

Note : The possessive Pronouns, such as "mērā", "hamārā", "tumhārā", "āpkā", "uskā", "unkā", etc., follow the same rules as Adjectives; as,

EXAMPLES

1.	He is a good boy.	Woh ach-chhā laṙkā hai.
2.	Your dog was in my room.	Tumhārā kutta mērē kamrē mēň thā.
3.	The large envelopes were on the small table.	Baṙē lifāfē chhoṭī mēz par thē.
4.	His servants were in the low rooms.	Uskē naukar nīchē kamroň mēň thē.
5.	My daughter was on the good mare.	Mērī bēṭī ach-chhī ghoṙī par thī.
6.	His sons were in the small carriages.	Uskē bēṭē chhoṭī garioň mēň thē.

EXERCISE 13(A)

1. Chhoṭā laṙkā baṙē kamrē mēň thā. 2. Ach-chhē lifāfē chhotī kitāb mēň haiň. 3. Tumhārī pagṙī bahut mailī hai. 4. Yeh pēṭī bahut lambī nahīň hai. 5. Barī mēzēň hamāṙē kamṙoň mēň haiň. 6. Chhoṭī dawāt mēň sīāhī nahīň hai. 7. Ach-chhē laṙkē kī māň baṙē ghoṙē par hai. 8. Mērī naī bandūq kī nālī sāf nahīň hai. 9. Naē sandūqoň kī chābīāň purānē kot (coat) kī jēb mēň hāiň. 10. Uňchē palaňg kī chādarēň bahut mailī haiň. 11. Is ādmī kī bīwī bāhut bīmār haī. 12. Is aurat kē bēṭē bāhut ach-chhē laṙkē haiň. 13. Ach-chhē kapṙē baṙē sandūqoň mēň haiň.

EXERCISE 13(B)

1. The good boy is in the large room. 2. The wet clothes are on the large table. 3. My new locks were in the large boxes. 4. Your new watch was in the low carriage. 5. His keys were in my pocket. 6. The little girls were on the good mares. 7. My brother's old servant is in your room. 8. The keys

of your office are in my son's pocket. 9. The old boxes are in the dirty houses. 10. My brother's servant is a good man. 11. The locks of your boxes are very old. 12. My servant's turbans are dirty. 13. A brother of my wife is a great liar. 14. Your new books were in the big boxes.

Adjectives					
Rich	Amīr	امیر	Poor	<u>Gh</u>arīb	غریب
Easy	Āsān	آسان	Difficult	Mushkil	مشکل
Well	Tan-durust	تندرست	Ill	Bīmār	بیمار
Wise	Aqlmand	عقل‌مند	Foolish	Bēwaqūf	بیوقوف
Hard	Sa<u>kh</u>t	سخت	Soft	Narm	نرم
Honest	Īmāndār	ایماندار	Dishonest	Bē-īmān	بے ایمان
Strong	Mazbūt	مضبوط	Weak	Kamzor	کمزور
Swift	Tēz	تیز	Cheap	Sastā	سستا
Sharp	Tēz	تیز	Blunt	Kund	کند
Active	Chālāk	چالاک	Lazy	Sust	سست
Beautiful	<u>Kh</u>ūbsūrat	خوبصورت	Ugly	Bad-sūrat	بدصورت
Slow	Dhīmā or halkā	ہلکا	Expensive	Mañhgā	مہنگا

The Degree of Comparison

There are three degrees of Adjectives in English; viz.,

The Positive	Comparative	Superlative
Large	Larger	Largest
Good	Better	Best
Strong	Stronger	Strongest
Bad	Worse	Worst
Beautiful	More beautiful	Most beautiful.

The Adjectives in Urdu have no Degrees of comparison corresponding to the above.

In Urdu the comparison between the two things is expressed by placing the Post-position "s ē" (which here means "compared with "or" than") after the Noun with which the comparison is made while the Adjective is made to agree with the Noun which is compared; as,

1. A horse is larger than a dog.
   (A horse, dog than, large is)—
   Ghoṙā kuttē sē baṙā haī.

2. The mare is dirtier than the dog.
   (Mare, dog than, dirty is)—
   Ghoṙī kuttē sē mailī haī.

3. The horses are higher than the carriages.
   (Horses, carriages than, high are)—
   Ghoṙē gāṙīoṅ sē ūṅchē haiṅ.

4. Your horse is cheaper than my mare.
   (Your horse, my mare than, cheap is)—
   Tumhārā ghoṙā mērī ghoṙī sē sasṭā hai.
   (or) Āpkā ghoṙā mērī ghoṙī sē sastā hai.

5. The matting is longer than the room.
   (Matting, room than, longer is)—
   Chaṭāī kamrē sē lambī haī.

6. The paper of the book is better than that of the newspaper.
   (Book's paper, newspaper's paper than, good is)—
   Kitāb kā kāghaz akhbār kē kāghaz sē ach-chha haī.

Superlative Degree

The superlative degree is expressed by using "sab se" (than all) before an ordinary Adjective; as,

Good	Ach-chhā	—	Best	Sab sē ach-chhā	سب سے اچھا
Bad	Kharāb	—	Worst	Sab sē kharāb	سب سے خراب
Large	Bařā	—	Largest	Sab sē bařā	سب سے بڑا
Small	Chhoṭā	—	Smallest	Sab sē chhoṭā	سب سے چھوٹا
Weak	Kamzor	—	Weakest	Sab sē kamzor.	سب سے کمزور

EXAMPLES

1. He was the best boy. (He, all than good, boy was)— Woh, sab sē ach-chhā, lařkā thā.

2. She is the wisest girl. (She, all than wise, girl is)— Woh, sab sē aqlmand, lařkī haī.

3. These are the cheapest locks. (These, all than cheap, locks are)— Yeh, sab sē sastē, tālē haiň.

4. This is the longest belt. Yeh, sab sē lambī, pēṭī haī.

5. That was the most beautiful watch. Woh, sab sē khūbsūrat ghařī thī.

EXERCISE 14(A)

1. Chhoṭī mēz bařī mēz sē maňhgī haī. 2. Hamārā naukar tumhārē bētē sē sust hai. 3. Is ādmī kā ghořā sab sē ach-chhā hai. 4. Mahmūd sāheb kā daftar Asghar sāheb kē daftar sā bařā haī. 5. Yeh bařā lařkā chhoṭī lařkī sē sust hai. 6. Darzī kī dukān qasāī kē ghar sē bařī haī. 7. Yeh bewaqūf ādmī tumhārē bāp sē aqlmand hai. 8. Yeh sab sē mushkil kitāb hai. 9. Tum gharīb ādmī ho; magar (but) mujh sē amīr ho. 10. Woh bařā ghanṭa is chhoṭī ghařī sē sastā

hai. 11. Woh mazbūt ādmī sab sē sust hai. 12. Sab sē lambī lakṛī mērē kamrē kē konē mēṅ hai. 13. In kitāboṅ mēṅ sab sē ach-chhī kitāb kaunsī hai? 14. Mērā nayā naukar tumhārē purānē naukar sē īmāndār aur aqlmand hai.

WORDS

Masculines					
Village	Gāoṅ	گاؤں	Way	Rāsta	راستہ
City	Shahr	شہر	Younger (*adj.*)	Chhoṭā	چھوٹا
Elder (*adj.*)	Baṛā	بڑا			
Feminines					
Road	Saṛak	سڑک	Chain	Zanjīr	زنجیر
Rope	Rassī	رسّی	Expensive	Maṅhgā	مہنگا
Footpath	Pagdandī	پگڈنڈی			

EXERCISE 14(B)

1. The Post Office is larger than the Telegraph Office. 2. The watch is smaller than the clock. 3. The envelopes are wider than the papers. 4. This cloth is wider than the small table. 5. A chain will be stronger than a rope. 6. The horses are higher than the carriages. 7. My room is cooler than your office. 8. Your sons are dirtier than my dog. 9. The husband of the women was taller than your brother. 10. Your daughter is older than his sister. 11. The chairs are older than the tables. 12. This is the largest box in my room. 13. This foolish man is the wisest man in this village. 14. Your shop is most expensive.

The Interrogative and Relative Pronouns etc.

1. When asking a question, if there is no word (such as "why", "what", etc.) which shows that the sentence is interrogative, either use the word "kiā" (what) at the beginning or simply raise the voice at the end.

Is that your horse ?

Kiā woh tumahārā ghoṙā hai? کیا وہ تمہارا گھوڑا ہے ؟

Is my book on the table ?

Mērī kitāb mēz par hai ? میری کتاب میز پر ہے ۔

The Interrogative Pronouns are used in asking questions, as, who is that man? Which is your book?

3. The Relative Pronouns are used in connecting two sentences or ideas, as, this is the man who was in my room. The book which is on my table is not yours.

In English the same words are used for Interrogatives and Relatives, as is seen from the examples in the above sub-clauses (2) and (3), but in Urdu they have two different words, the uses of which are explained in the following rules.

4. When using the words, "who", "when", "what", etc., use one of the Interrogative (question) Form if you expect an answer, their respective Relative Forms given against them in the following list.

Note :— The Relatives are formed by changing the initial "K" of the Interrogatives into "J" as will be seen in the following list.

Interrogatives			Relatives	
Who	Kaun	کون	Jo (Exception)	جو
Whose	Kis kā	کس کا	Jis kā	جس کا
To whom	Kis ko	کس کو	Jis ko	جس کو
Which	Kaunsā	کونسا	Jo (exception)	جو
What	Kīā	کیا	Jo (exception)	جو
Where	Kahāň	کہاں	Jahāň	جہاں
When	Kab	کب	Jab	جب
What sort of	Kaisā	کیسا	Jaisā	جیسا
How (in what manner)	Kaisē	کیسے	Jaisē	جیسے
How much	Kitnā, Kitnī	کتنا، کتنی	Jitnā, Jitnī	جتنا، جتنی
How many	Kitnā, Kitnī	〃	Jitnā, Jitnī	〃
How far	Kitnī dūr	کتنی دور	Jitnī dur	جتنی دور
How long (time)	Kitnī dēr	کتنی دیر	Jitnī dēr	جتنی دیر
Why	Kīoň	کیوں	—	

Note :— **The rules for the uses of Interrogatives are given on page 21.**

EXAMPLES

1. Who is that man? — Woh ādmī kaun hai?
2. Where is his house? — Uskā ghar kahāň hai?
3. What is the name of your father? — Tūmhārē bāp kā nām kiā hai?
4. Where is the key of my small box? — Mērē chhoṭē sandūq kī chābī kahāň hai?

5.	How many men were in the carriage?	Gāṛī mēṅ kitnē ādmī thē?
6.	This is the book which was on my table.	Yeh woh kitāb hai, jo mērī mēz par thī.
7.	I was at Delhi when you were at Lahore.	Maiṅ Delhi mēṅ thā, jab tum Lahore mēṅ thē.

EXERCISE 15(A)

1. Baṛē kamrē mēṅ kaun hai? 2. Tumhārṅ kamrē mēṅ kiskā bēṭā hai ? 3. Hamārī ṭopī kaunsē sandūq mēṅ hai ? 4. Yeh chhoṭi kitāb kaisī hai ? 5. Chhoṭē sandūq mēṅ kitnē andē haiṅ? 6. Tumhārē bēṭē kē naukar kē ghar dāk khānē sē kitnī dūr hai? 7. Is kamrē mēṅ kitnī kursīāṅ haiṅ 8. Chhāonī ko kaunsā rāsta jata hai? 9. In kitāboṅ mēṅ kaunsī kitāb sab sē ach-chhī hai? 10. Chhoṭī kitāb, jo mērī mēz par hai, bahut mushkil hai. 11. Woh ādmī, jiskā ghoṛā darakht kē nīchē hai, chor hai. 12. Jab woh ādmī aur aurat bāzār mēṅ thē, maiṅ uskī dukān mēṅ thā. 13. yeh kaunsē tālē kī chābī hai?

EXERCISE 15(B)

1. What is the name of your new servant? 2. Who is on my horse? 3. Where is that boy's house? 4. What are his sons' names? 5. Whose son are you? 6. How are you? 7. Which is the coolest room? 8. On which horse was your daughter? 9. When was my dog in your room? 10. What is the price of this watch? 11. Why were you not in the office? 12. What sort of carriages are those? 13. How much ink was in the inkpot? 14. How far is the Post Office from the Telegraph Office? 15. The man, who was in your room is my brother. 16. I was in the office when you were in the carriage. 17. This is the man whose son was your servant. 18. Where were you when I was in the room? 19. Is this your hat or mine?

Substantives used as Post-positions

On account of	kē sabab	کے سبب
Under, below	kē nīchē	کے نیچے
Behind	kē pīchhē	کے پیچھے
For	kē wāstē or kē līē	کے واسطے / کے لیے
Without	kē baghair	کے بغیر
With	kē sāth	کے ساتھ
In the middle of	kē bīch mēň	کے بیچ میں
Between	kē darmīān	کے درمیان
Instead of	kē badlē	کے بدلے
Beyond	kē parē	کے پرے
According to	kē muāfiq	کے موافق
Round	kē gird	کے گرد
Round about	kē ās pās	کے آس پاس
In front of	kē sāmnē	کے سامنے
Before (ahead)	kē āgē	کے آگے
Before (in time)	sē pahlē	سے پہلے
After (in time)	kē bād	کے بعد
Inside	kē andar	کے اندر
Outside	kē bāhar	کے باہر
Against	kē khilāf	کے خلاف
Across	kē pār	کے پار
	kē qarīb, or	کے قریب
Near	kē nazdīk, or	کے نزدیک
	kē pās	کے پاس

The following are connected with the preceding Noun by means of "kī"—

Towards	kī taraf	کی طرف	Like	kī tarah	کی طرح
For the sake of	kī khātir	کی خاطر	About (concerning)	kī bābat	کی بابت

The above Substantives in Urdu are used in place of Post-positions. Such substantives are used after the Nouns which they govern, and are connected with them by the inflected "Kē" or "K ī" — "of" (according to whether they are Masculine or Feminine.)

Note :— A similar construction is found in English. Thus "Kē nazdīk" might be translated by "in the neighbourhood of" and "K ē pīchhē" by "in the rear of".

EXAMPLES

Near the village (in the vicinity of the village)
Gāoṅ kē nazdīk گاؤں کے نزدیک

Behind the house (In the rear of the house)
Ghar kē pīchhē گھر کے پیچھے

With the horse (In company of the horse)
Ghoṛē kē sāth گھوڑے کے ساتھ

Towards the room (In the direction of the room)
Kamrē kī taraf کمرے کی طرف

Concerning or (about) the servant
Naukar ki babat نوکر کی بابت

Observation. — **Since "men" or some other Post-position is understood after such words as "nazdīk, pīchhē, sath" etc., the "k ā" before them is used in the inflected form.**

Note : — When a Pronoun is governed by such Substantives, the "kē" or "kī" is omitted and the Possessive Form of the Pronoun is used; as,

Near me (in my vicinity) — Mere qarīb (not "mujh Kē qarīb" or "Mērē Kē qarīb").

With you (in your company)— Tumhārē sāth (not "tum kē sāth" or "tumhārē kē sāth").

Towards us (In our direction — Hamārī taraf (not Ham kī taraf or Hamari kī taraf").

With him (In his company) — Uskē sāth (not "usko kē sāth").

EXAMPLES

1.	The man was on the horse.	Ādmī ghořē par thā.
2.	My dog was under the table.	Mērā kuttā mēz kē nīchē thā.
3.	He was here without my order.	Woh yahāň mērē hukm kē bag<u>h</u>air thā.
4.	The boy's house is outside the city.	Lařkē kā ghar shahr kē bāhar hai.
5.	There is a beautiful chain with the watch.	Ghařī kē sāth ēk <u>kh</u>ūbsūrat zanjīr hai.
6.	There were five men in my room.	Mērē kamrē kē andar pāňch ādmı thē.
7.	The guns were behind the boxes.	Bandūqēň sandūqoň kē pīchhē thīň.
8.	The horses were for the boys, and the mares for the girls.	Ghořē lařkoň kē wāstē thē aur ghořīāň lařkīoň kē wāstē thīň.
9.	My son will be with me.	Mērā bēţā mērē sāth hogā.
10.	This beautiful watch is for you.	Yeh <u>kh</u>ūbsūrat ghařī tumhārē wāstē hai.
11.	There was a high wall in front of them.	Unkē sāmnē ēk ūňchī dīwār thī.
12.	There is a large garden round my brother's house.	Mērē bhāī kē ghar kē gird ēk bařā bāg<u>h</u> hai.

EXERCISE 16(A)

1. Mērī dukān tār ghar kē nazdīk hai. 2. Mērā nām tumhārē nām kē nīchē hai. 3. Rassī zanjīr kē nīchē thī. 4. Tumhārī lakṛī baṛē sandūq kē pīchhē hai. 5. Kīā yeh sust naukar mērē dost kē wāstē hai. 6. Laṛkē īskūl mēn̈ kitābon̈ kē baghair thē 7. Darzī kē sāth uskā naukar thā. 8. Tumhārē ghar kē sāmnē kitnē ādmī thē. 9. Khazānē kē gird bahut ādmī thē. 10. Ghoṛē kē sāth ēk purānī zīn hai. 11. Do chor gāṛī kē sāmnē aur do chor gāṛī kē pīchhē thē. 12. Is gāon̈ kē ās pās shikār nahīn̈ hai. 13. Darzī dukān kē bāhar thā aur uskā naukar dukān kē andar thā. 14. Us ādmī kī bētī dīwār kī taraf thī.

Masculines					
Snake	Sān̈p	سانپ	Enemy	Dushman	دشمن
Knowledge	Ilm	علم	Thief	Chor	چور
Bungalow	Ban̈gla	بنگلہ	Soldier	Sipāhī	سپاہی
River	Daryā	دریا	Tree	Pēṛ or darakht	پیڑ/درخت
Feminines					
Wealth	Daulat	دولت	Neglect	Ghaflat	غفلت
Opinion	Rāē	رائے	Land	Zamīn	زمین
Help	Madad	مدد	Punishment	Sazā	سزا
Mess	Mess	میس	Wine	Sharāb	شراب
Cow	Gāē	گائے	Train	Rēlgāṛī	ریل گاڑی

EXERCISE 16(B)

1. My house is near the Post Office. 2. Here is a large snake behind the box. 3. My brother's horse was under the tree. 4. What is wealth without knowledge. 5. Is there any letter for me? 6. This is on account of your neglect. 7. Whose servant was with you? 8. The treasury is beyond the hospital. 9. The carriage was in front of my shop. 10. The soldiers were outside the village. 11. It is against the Major's order. 12. The thieves were

inside the room. 13. The mess is beyond the Post Office. 14. Who was with the Adjutant? 15. The mares were under the large trees. 16. My bungalow is near the Telegraph Office. 17. The servants were with the carriages.

Words

An hour	Ghanṭā	گھنٹہ	Day	Din or roz	دن / روز
Week	Hafta	ہفتہ	Fortnight	Do Haftē	دو ہفتے
Month	Mahīna	مہینہ	Year	Sāl or baras	سال / برس
Night	Rāt	رات	To-day	Āj	آج
To-night	Āj rāt ko	آج رات کو	Morning	Subah	صبح
Evening	Shām	شام	Noon	Do pahar	دوپہر
Afternoon	Tīsrē pahar	تیسرے پہر	At sun-rise	Din nikle	دن نکلے
At sun-set	Din chhupē	دن چھپے	At midnight	Ādhī rāt ko	آدھی رات کو
Every	Har	ہر	Once	Ēk dafa	ایک دفعہ
Twice	Do dafa	دو دفعہ	This morning	Āj subah ko	آج صبح کو
This evening	Āj sham ko	آج شام کو	Last week	Pichhlē haftē	پچھلے ہفتے
Next week	Aglē haftē	اگلے ہفتے	Early	Sawērē	سویرے
Yesterday	Kal	کل	Tomorrow	Kal	کل
Any	Koī	کوئی	Several	Kaī	کئی
No-one	Koī nahīṅ	کوئی نہیں			
Tomorrow night		Last night		Kal Raat Ko	کل رات کو
Day before Yesterday	Parsoṅ	پرسوں	Day after Tomorrow	Parsoṅ	پرسوں

REVISIONAL EXERCISE 17(A)

(On Exercises from 12 to 16)

1. What is the price of that land which is in front of your bungalow?

2. Do not cross the river without a gun this morning. 3. He was here with a friend before 8 o'clock last night. 4. A wise enemy is better than a foolish friend. 5. This old wine is good for that old man. 6. Yesterday was the coldest day of this month. 7. The little boy who is under the tree is the eldest son of my friend. 8. Whom is this letter for? 9. What is your opinion about it to-day? 10. This is the largest village between the two cities. 11. The boys and girls, who are sons and daughters today, will be fathers and mothers tomorrow.

REVISIONAL EXERCISE 17(B)

Read, write and translate into English.

۱۔ یہ سب سے اچھا آدمی ہے۔ ۲۔ تمہارا گھر میرے گھر سے بڑا ہے۔ ۳۔ اس آدمی کا دوست تار گھر میں ہے۔ ۴۔ دفتر کے تالوں کی چابیاں علی صاحب کے کمرے کو لے جاؤ۔ ۵۔ احمد صاحب کے نوکر کے بیٹے کے صندوق کی چابی ڈرائیور کے جیب میں تھی۔ ۶۔ اس آدمی کی بیوی بہت بیمار ہے۔ ۷۔ اس عورت کے بیٹے بہت اچھے لڑکے ہیں۔ ۸۔ اچھے کپڑے بڑے صندوق میں ہیں۔ ۹۔ ان کتابوں میں سب سے اچھی کتاب کون سی ہے۔ ۱۰۔ میرا نیا نوکر تمہارے پرانے نوکر سے ایماندار اور عقلمند ہے۔ ۱۱۔ وہ آدمی جس کی موٹر کار درخت کے نیچے کھڑی ہے بہت اچھا ہے۔ ۱۲۔ جب وہ آدمی اور عورت بازار میں تھے میں اس دوکان میں تھا۔ ۱۳۔ درزی دوکان کے اندر تھا اور اس کا نوکر دکان کے باہر تھا۔ ۱۴۔ ان عورتوں کے خاوند کلب میں تھے اور ان کی بیٹیاں اسکولوں میں تھیں۔

REVISIONAL EXERCISE 17(C)

Read, write and translate into English.

۱۔ وہ زمین جو تمہارے بنگلے کے سامنے ہے اُس کی قیمت کیا ہے ؟
۲۔ آج شام کو لکڑی کے بغیر جنگل کے پار مت جاؤ۔ ۳۔ وہ
ایک دوست کے ساتھ آج صبح یہاں تھا۔ ۴۔ اُس بوڑھے
آدمی کے لیے روٹی لاؤ۔ ۵۔ کل اس مہینے کا سب سے گرم
دن تھا۔ ۶۔ وہ لڑکا جو باغ میں ہے میرے دوست کا سب
سے بڑا بیٹا ہے۔ ۷۔ یہ خط کس کے واسطے ہے ؟ ۸۔ اس
کی بابت آپ کی رائے کیا ہے ؟ ۹۔ کراچی پاکستان کا سب
ے بڑا شہر ہے۔ ڈھاکہ ہمارا سب سے ریادہ خوبصورت
شہر ہے۔ ۱۰۔ وہ لڑکے اور لڑکیاں جو آج بیٹے اور بیٹیاں
ہیں کل باپ اور ماں ہوں گے۔

THE ADVERBS

The Adverbs are of several kinds, most of which are given below under different headings.

Now	Ab	اب	Always	Hamēsha	ہمیشہ
Just now	Abhī	ابھی	Quickly	Jaldī sē	جلدی سے
Yet	Abhī tak	ابھی تک	Soon	Jaldī	جلدی
Again, then	Phīr	پھر	Ever	Kabhī	کبھی
In future	Āīnda	آئندہ	Never	Kabhī nahīň	کبھی نہیں
Every day	Har roz	ہر روز	Suddenly	Achānak	اچانک
Now-a-days	Āj kal	آج کل	In turns	Bārī bārī	باری باری
Often	Aksar	اکثر	At present	Filhāl	فی الحال

Adverbs of Place

Everywhere	Har jagah	ہر جگہ
No where	Kahin nahīň	کہیں نہیں
By sea	Sumandar kē rāstē	سمندر کے راستے
By land	Khushki kē rāstē	خشکی کے راستے
By air	Hawāī jahāz sē	ہوائی جہاز سے

Adverbs of Quantity

A little	Thořā	تھوڑا	Alone	Akēlā	اکیلا
Even	Bhī	بھی	Enough	Kāfī	کافی
Only	Sirf	صرف	Some	Kuchh	کچھ

Adverbs of Affirmation

Yes	Jī haṅ	جی ہاں	Undoubtedly	Bēshak	بیشک
Certainly	Zarūr	ضرور	or Indeed		

Adverbs of Negation

No, Not	Nahīṅ	نہیں	Otherwise	Warna	ورنہ
Not at all	Bilkul nahīṅ	بالکل نہیں		or nahīṅ to	نہیں تو

The following Arabic Adverbs are commonly used in Urdu

At once	Fauran	فوراً	About (nearly)	Taqrīban	تقریباً
Per force	Majbūran	مجبوراً	By force	Jabran	جبراً
For example	Māslan	مثلاً	By chance	Ittifāqan	اتفاقاً
probably	<u>Gh</u>āliban	غالباً	Especially	<u>Kh</u>usūsan	خصوصاً
Surely	Yaqīnan	یقیناً	Approximately	Ta<u>kh</u>mīnan	تخمیناً
Commonly / Usually	Umūman	عموماً			

The Conjunction

A conjunction is a word, which is used to connect two words or sentences; as,

And	Aur	اور	That	Keh	کہ
Or	Yā	یا	If	Agar	اگر
But	Lēkin	لیکن	Also, even	Bhī	بھی
However	Magar	مگر	Yet (even then)	Phir bhī	پھر بھی
Because	Kīoṅkeh	کیونکہ	Although	Agarcheh	اگرچہ
Since	Chūṅkeh	چونکہ	therefore	Is līē	اس لیے
According	Chunāṅcheh	چنانچہ	Likewise	Is hī tarah	اسی طرح

The Interjunction

O! "O" or "Ai"		او / ارے	Hurrah	Wāh Wāh	واہ واہ
Well done Bravo	Shābāsh	شاباش	Is it really?	Kiā such much	کیا سچ مچ
Eh! what!	Haiň — !	ہیں	Be careful	Khabardār	خبردار

THE VERB

There are two principal kinds of Verbs, viz., Transitive and Intransitive.

(a) A verb is Transitive, if the action has an object without which the sense would be incomplete; as

The dog killed a fox. I saw a man.

Here the sense would be incomplete without mentioning "fox" and "man" and therefore the Verbs "kill" and "see" are both Transitive.

(b) A Verb is Intransitive if the action does not pass to an Object; as,

The servant is sleeping. The boy ran.

Here the sense is already complete without placing any objects after the Verbs "sleep" or "run". They are therefore Intransitive.

Note :— **The Transitive and Intransitive Verbs differ in their use only in the Past Tense.**

The Infinitive

The Infinitive expresses only the action or state and is not limited as regards person, number and time; as,

To come,. To cut, To fall, To write, etc.

As in English every Infinitive is preceded by "To" so in the same way every Infinitive in Urdu terminates in "n ā"

Infinitives

Intransitives			**Transitives**		
To come	Ānā	آنا	To see	Dēkhnā	دیکھنا
To go	Jānā	جانا	To show	Dikhānā	دکھانا
To sleep	Sonā	سونا	To eat	Khānā	کھانا
To walk	Chalnā	چلنا	To drop	Girānā	گرانا
To wake (one self)	Jāgnā	جاگنا	To awaken	Jagānā	جگانا
To speak	Bolnā	بولنا	To call	Bulānā	بلانا
To lie down	Lēṭnā	لیٹنا	To change	Badalnā	بدلنا
To laugh	Haňsnā	ہنسنا	To write	Likhnā	لکھنا
To bring	Lānā	لانا	To drink	Pīnā	پینا
To sit	Baiṭhnā	بیٹھنا	To open	Kholnā	کھولنا
To wait	Thaīrnā	ٹھہرنا	To shut	Band karnā	بند کرنا
To fall	Girnā	گرنا	To give	Dēnā	دینا
To rise	Uṭhnā	اُٹھنا	To send	Bhējnā	بھیجنا
To arrive or To reach	Pahuňchnā	پہنچنا	To raise To lift up To pick up	Uṭhānā	اٹھانا
To climb To mount To get on	Chaṙhnā	چڑھنا	To keep To put To place	Rakhnā	رکھنا
To take away or To carry	Lējānā	لے جانا	To say, To tell	Kahnā	کہنا

THE IMPERATIVE

The Urdu Verbs are quite simple and regular in form and it wants but little practice to form any particular part or tense of a Verb, if we know the Infinitive of it.

(a) The root of a Verb is obtained by omitting the final "nā" of the Infinitive; as,

To go	Jānā	—	Root	Jā	جا
To speak	bolnā	—	Root	Bol	بول

(b) The Imperative or "word of command" is formed by adding "o" to the root of a Verb; as,

			Root	**Imperative**	
To speak	Bolnā	—	Bol	Bolo	بولو
To strike	Mārnā	—	Mār	Māro	مارو
To drop	Girānā	—	Girā	Girāo	گراؤ

Note:— If the root ends either in "e" or "o", these vowels are dropped, for the sake of euphony, before the termination "o" of the Imperative; as,

			Root	**Imperative**
To give	Dēnā	—	Dē	Do
To sleep	Sonā	—	So	So

EXAMPLES

1.	Come into the room	Kamrē mēn̆ āo.
2.	Bring my horse.	Mera ghoṙā lāo.
3.	Take all things away.	Sab chīzēn̆ lējāo.
4.	Open that box.	Woh snadūq kholo.
5.	Put that paper in my pocket	Woh kāghaz mērī jēb mēn̆ rakho.
6.	Send this letter to the mess	Yeh chiṭṭhī mess ko bhējo.

Prohibition is expressed by using the particle "mat" — "do not" or "don't" before the Imperative; as,

1. Do not (or don't) go to the mess today. Āj mess ko mat jāo.
2. Don't sit on the chair. Kursī par mat baitho
3. Don't put the bottle under the table. Botal mēz kē nīchē mat rakho.
4. Don't open his room. Uskā kamra mat kholo.
5. Don't climb up that tree. Us darakht par mat chaṙho.

EXERCISE 18(A)

1. Bīmār ādmī kē kamrē mēṅ jāo. 2. Āj shām ko hamārē kapṙē klab ko lējāo. 3. Hamārē ghar ko do bajē sē pahlē āo. 4. Yeh chiṭṭhī jaldī sē Amjad sāheb kē daftar ko lējāo. 5. Das bajē kē bād barāmdē mēṅ mat chalo. 6. Yeh sandūq afsar kē sāmnē kholo. 7. Dhobī ko bulāo aur hamārē mailē kapṙē us ko do. 8. Dāk khānē ko jāo aur hamārī chiṭṭhīāṅ lāo. 9. Mērē kamrē kē andar baitho aur dākṭar sāhēb kē wāstē ṭhairo. 10. Saṙak kē bīch mēṅ mat baiṭho. 11. Yeh sab chīzēṅ uṭhāo aur yahāṅ sē ēk-dam jāo. 12. Mēz kā kapṙa jaldī sē badlo. 13. Yeh sandūq mērē hukm kē baghair mat kholo. 14. Yeh khat Smith sāheb kē baṅglē ko lējāo

WORDS

Masculines			Feminines		
Answer	Jawāb	جواب	Needle	Sūī	سوئی
Razor	Ustarā	اُسترا	Scissors	Qaīṅchī	قینچی
Lid	Dhaknā	ڈھکنا	Sleeve	Āstīn	آستین
Sock	Moza	موزہ	String	Sutlī	سُتلی
Glove	Dastāna	دستانہ	Cord	Ḍorī	ڈوری
Telegram	Tār	تار	Merry (*adj.*)	Khush	خوش
Letter	Khat	خط	All (*adj.*)	Sab	سب

EXERCISE 18(B)

1. Bring an answer from the gentleman. 2. Come here next week. 3. Don't go there tomorrow morning. 4. Change the sheet of my bed every day. 5. Put all these things in that carriage. 6. Give me my gloves. 7. Lift up the lid of this box. 8. Write his name on this envelope. 9. Give this book to my brother. 10. Open that door at once. 11. Wait on the verandah for an answer. 12. Don't laugh in front of me. 13. Bearer, come here, there is a large snake behind the box, kill it with a stick. 14. Take away all the things from the table. 15. Don't mount (on) that horse. 16. Get us tea very early tomorrow morning. 17. Eat, drink and be merry.

The use of the Preposition "to"

The preposition "to" must be translated by "k ē pās" (and not by "ko) when it is used before a human being (or a Pronoun), with any of the following Verbs, (which it will be noticed, involve movement from one place to another):—

Jānā	To go	جانا	Lānā	To bring	لانا
Ānā	To come	آنا	Lējānā	To take to	لے جانا
Bhējnā	To send	بھیجنا	Pahuṅchnā	To reach	پہنچنا

Note :— Before inanimate objects "to" takes its ordinary form "ko"

EXAMPLES

1. Go to the Post Master.
   Post Masṭer sāheb kē pās jāo. پوسٹ ماسٹر صاحب کے پاس جاؤ

2. Go to the Post Office.
   Ḍāk khāne ko jāo. ڈاکخانہ کو جاؤ

3. Take this letter to my son.
   Yeh khat mērē bēṭē kē pās lējāo. یہ خط میرے بیٹے کے پاس لے جاؤ

4. Come to me tomorrow morning.
Kal subah mērē pās āo.
کل صبح میرے پاس آؤ

5. Come to my house the day after tomorrow.
Parsoṅ mērē ghar ko āo.
پرسوں میرے گھر کو آؤ

6. Send this saddle to him.
Yeh zīn uskē pās bhējo.
یہ زین اس کے پاس بھیجو

7. Do not bring the car to me today.
Āj kār mērē pās mat lāo.
آج کار میرے پاس مت لاؤ

EXERCISE 19(A)

1. Is ādmī kē sāth darzī kē pās jāo. 2. Tum yeh khat Mahmood sāheb kē pās bhējo. 3. Āj Itwār hai, āj us kē pās mat jāo. 4. Yeh ghořā āj shām ko mērē pās lāo. 5. Do ādmī aur tīn lařkē Alī sāheb kē baṅglē ko bhējo. 6. Hamārē sab jānwar gāoṅ sē shahr ko lāo. 7. Is lařkī ko uskē khāwind kē pās bhējo. 8. Is ghařī kī qīmat hamārī dukān ko bhējo. 9. Yeh chiṭṭhī us ādmī kē pās wāpas lējāo. 10. Hamārē hukm kē baghair Post Master sāheb kē pās mat jāo. 11. Yeh sab chīzēṅ hamārē dost kē pās lējāo. 12. Woh taswīrēṅ bank kē bābū kē pās bhējo.

EXERCISE 19(B)

1. Send this shirt to the tailor. 2. Send this telegram to the office. 3. Do not go to him today. 4. Take this letter to Mr. Lloyd George. 5. Bring that sword to me in the office. 6. Come to my father next week. 7. Come to my bungalow tomorrow evening. 8. Take these chairs to the office. 9. Send a man to the Doctor. 10. Go to the butcher's house, if he is not in the shop. 11. Bring those eggs to me. 12. Send this horse to my friend.

INFINITIVES

Intransitives			Transitives		
To run	Daurnā	دوڑنا	To hear	Sunnā	سُننا
To die	Marnā	مرنا	To know	Jānnā	جاننا
To flow	Bahnā	بہنا	To cut	Kāṭnā	کاٹنا
To come out	Nikalnā	نکلنا	To take out	Nīkālnā	نکالنا
To fly	Uṙnā	اُڑنا	To fill	Bharnā	بھرنا
To live	Rahnā	رہنا	To understand	Samajhnā	سمجھنا
To be angry	<u>Kh</u>afā honā	خفا ہونا	To work	Kām karnā	کام کرنا
To do	Karnā	کرنا	To take	Lēnā	لینا
To smile	Muskurānā	مسکرانا	To throw	Phēṅknā	پھینکنا
To burn	Jalnā	جلنا	To make	Banānā	بنانا
To read	Paṙhnā	پڑھنا	To ask	Pūchhnā	پوچھنا
To become	Hojānā	ہوجانا	To clean	Sāf karnā	صاف کرنا
To sell	Bēchnā	بیچنا	To be , To have	Honā	ہونا
To swim	Tairnā	تیرنا	To take off	Utārnā	اُتارنا
To escape (from punishment etc.)	Bachnā	بچنا	To burn To light	Jalānā	جلانا
To escape (from danger etc.)	Bhāgnā	بھاگنا	To buy	<u>Kh</u>arīdnā or Mol lēnā	خریدنا یا مول لینا
To advance To come forward	Āgē baṙhnā آگے بڑھنا		To strike To hit To beat	Mārnā	مارنا
To retreat, To get back	Pīchhē haṭnā پیچھے ہٹنا		To kill To prepare	Mār-dālnā Taiyār karnā	مارڈالنا تیار کرنا
To weep, To cry	Ronā	رونا	To get ready	Taiyār honā	تیار ہونا
To shout, To cry To scream	Chil-lānā	چلّانا	To steal To break	Churānā Toṙnā	چُرانا توڑنا
To get down To dismount	Utarnā	اُترنا	To put on To teach	Pahennā Sikhānā	پہننا سکھانا

Present Participle

Present Particile is formed by adding "tā" or "rah ā" to the root of a verb; as,

			Root	Present Participle	Meaning
To speak	Bolnā	—	Bol	Boltā Bol rahā	Speaks Speaking
To go	Jānā	—	Jā	Jātā Jā rahā	Goes Going

Note :— (1) "ta" added to the root, denotes that the action takes place generally or as a habit; as, goes, sleeps, drinks.

(2) "raha" added to the root denotes action going on at the moment; as, is going, is sleeping, is drinking.

Practice

Form the Present Participles of all the Verbs given in the list on page 74 and 75 first by adding "tā" and then "rah ā".

Present Tense

The Present Tense is of two kinds; e.g.,

(1) Present Indicative (or Indefinite)

(2) Present Continuous (or Definite).

1. Present Indicative (or Indefinite) shows that the action takes place or happens generally (not necessarily at some definite moment). It is Indefinite as regards time and may even be habitual; as,

(i) My sāheb speaks Urdu.

(ii) The tailor makes my suits.

In the above sentences "speaks" and "makes" show that the action takes place as a rule (not necessarily at the moment). These will be expressed by the Present Participles formed by adding "tā"; as, Boltā, Banātā, etc.

2. Present Continuous (or difinite) Tense is used when we wish to define more precisely the exact moment at which a certain action is going on; as,

(i) Look ! the sun is rising.

(ii) The saheb is speaking to a friend.

In the above sentences "rising" and "speaking" show that the action is taking place just now, and is not completed yet. They will be expressed by adding "rahā" as, "Nikal rah ā", "Bol rah ā".

Note :— "Rahā" is the Past-Participle of "Rahn ā", to remain, to be (in the act or state of).

MODEL CONJUGATIONS

Present Indicative (or Indefinite)

Singular		Plural	
I go	Maiṅ jātā hūṅ	We go	Ham jātē haiṅ
Thou goest	Tū jātā hai	You go	Tum jātē ho
He goes	Woh jātā hai	They go	Woh jātē haiṅ
She goes	Woh jātī hai	They go (*f.*)	Woh jātī haiṅ

Present Continuous (or Definite)

Singular		
I am going	Maiṅ jā rahā hūṅ	میں جارہا ہوں
Thou art going	Tū jā rahā hai	تو جارہا ہے
He is going	Woh jā rahā hai	وہ جارہا ہے
She is going	Who jā rahī hai	وہ جارہی ہے

Plural		
We are going	Ham jā rahē haiṅ	ہم جا رہے ہیں
You are going	Tum jā rahē ho	تم جا رہے ہو
They are going	Woh jā rahē haiṅ	وہ جا رہے ہیں
They are going (*f.*)	Woh jā rahī haiṅ	وہ جا رہی ہیں

Practice

Conjugate like the above Model Conjugations the following verbs, Khānā, Pīnā, Sonā, Dēkhnā and Chalnā.

Past Imperfect Tense

Like the Present Tense, the Past Imperfect is also of two kinds, e.g., the Definite the Indefinite as will be seen from the following conjugations:—

Past Imperfect (Indefinite)

I, He, etc. was going (usually)

Singular		Plural	
Maiṅ jātā thā	میں جاتا تھا	Ham jātē thē	ہم جاتے تھے
Tū jātā thā	تو جاتا تھا	Tum jātē thē	تم جاتے تھے
Woh jātā thā	وہ جاتا تھا	Woh jātē thē	وہ جاتے تھے
Woh jātī thī (*she*)	وہ جاتی تھی	Woh jātī thiṅ (*f.*)	وہ جاتی تھیں

Past Imperfect (Definite)

Singular		Plural	
Main jā rahā thā	میں جا رہا تھا	Ham jā rahē thē	ہم جا رہے تھے
Tū jā rahā thā	تو جا رہا تھا	Tum jā rahē thē	تم جا رہے تھے
Woh jā rahā thā	وہ جا رہا تھا	Woh jā rahē thē	وہ جا رہے تھے
Woh jā rahī thī (*she*)	وہ جا رہی تھی	Woh jā rahī thiṅ (*f.*)	وہ جا رہی تھیں

Formation of a Sentence

1st — The Position of the Nominative or the subject, with all its' "enlargements", is at the very beginning of a sentence, as it is in English.

2nd — The Position of the Object with all its "enlargements" is after the subject.

3rd — The Verb with all its "enlargements" is placed at the extreme end of the sentence.

Note:— (1) The enlargements of a Noun are the Adjective and the Possessive Pronouns; as, *My good* horse.

Note :— (2) The enlargements of a Verb are the Adverbs; as, He was *badly* wounded. The child is *not* sleeping.

Note : — (3) The enlargements must be used before their respective Nouns or Verbs, as in English.

EXAMPLES

1. The man was going to the office.
   (man, office to, going was)—
   Ādmī daftar ko jātā thā. (Indefinite)
   Ādmī daftar ko jā rahā thā (Definite)

2. His brother was sleeping in the small room.

His brother	small room in	sleeping was
Uskā bhāī,	chhoṭē kamrē mēṅ,	so rahā thā.

3. My servant is not reading your book.

My servant	your book	not reading is
Mērā naukar,	āp kī kitāb,	nahīṅ paṛh rahā hai.

4. I am not writing any letter now.

I	any letter	now not writing am
Maiň,	koī chiṭṭhī,	ab nahīň likh rahā hūň.

5. He always brings my tea late.

He	my tea	always late	brings
Woh,	mērī chāē,	hamēsha dēr sē,	lātā hai.

EXERCISE 20(A)

Gosht	Meat	گوشت	<u>Kh</u>ūb (*adv.*)	Well	خوب
Kām	Work	کام	Pahlē (*adv.*)	First	پہلے
Hajjām	Barber	حجام			

1. Tum kiā bēchtē ho? 2. Maiň qasāī hūň aur gosht bēchtā hūň. 3. Hajjām subah ko dukān kholtā hai aur shām ko band kartā hai. 4. Maiň dēkhtā hūň keh woh ādmī mērē baňglē ko hamēsha ātē haiň. 5. Tum unhēň (or unko) kioň nahīň roktē ho? 6. Mērē dost kē bēṭē har mahīnē do dafa shikār ko jātē haiň. 7. Yeh ādmī bahut achchhā kām kartā hai. 8. Tum is ādmī ko jāntē ho? 9. Main usē (or usko) <u>Kh</u>ūb jāntā hūň? 10. Woh pahlē hoṭel mēň rahtā thā, ab klab kē qarīb ēk baňgle mēň rahtā hai. 11. Main <u>kh</u>at kē jawāb hamēsha fauran dētā hūň. 12. Uskī bīwī har roz shām ko ṭēnis khēltī thī, āp kioň nahīň khēltī haiň?

EXERCISE 20(B)

Fort	Qila	قلعہ	Child	Bach-cha	بچہ
Sun	Sūraj	سورج	Sight	Tamāsha	تماشہ

1. He comes to me in the morning, I go to him in the evening, then we go to the club, and play tennis. 2. I do not buy anything from his shop. 3. My servant never steals anything. 4. Do you live in the front. 5. We do not see him everyday. 6. What time do you rise in the morning? 7. I rise when the sun rises. 8. Sometimes this man laughs, sometimes he cries, and sometimes he plays like a child. 9. She was writing letters to me now and then, but now she does not send any; I do not know (that) why? 10. My servants understand English well, but I speak Urdu to them. 11. You see that thing everyday and yet you do not know its name. 12. What does he do in the evening.?

WORDS

Phūl	Flower	پھول	Nāchnā	To dance	ناچنا
Pul	Bridge	پُل	Bhauṅknā	To bark	بھونکنا
Hawāī jahāz	Aeroplane	ہوائی جہاز	Kē ūpar	Over	کے اوپر

EXERCISE 21(A)

1. Maiṅ yeh pūchh rahā hun, keh tum mērā sandūq kīoṅ khol rahē thē? 2. Yeh ādmī yahāṅ kiā kar rahā hai? 3. Tum kahāṅ jā rahē ho? 4. Sab naukar barāmdē mēṅ haṅs rahē thē. 5. Dēkho sūraj nikal rahā hai aur tum abhī tak so rahē ho. 6. Yeh laṙkē kīā lējā rahē haiṅ? 7. Ghoṙā ṭhīk chal rahā hai, tum usē (us ko) kīoṅ mār rahē ho? 8. Laṙkē likh rahē thē, lēkin laṙkīāṅ khēl rahī thīṅ. 9. Gāē phūl khā rahī hai, aur kuttā us par bhauṅk rahā hai. 10. Sāīs ghoṙā taiyār kar rahā hai. 11. Us waqt shahr kē ūpar ēk hawāī jahāz uṙ rahā thā, aur sab log usē dēkh rahē thē. 12. Tum kiā dēkh rahē ho, yahān koī tamāsha ho rahā hai, yā koī nāch rahā hai?

EXERCISE 21(B)

People	Log	لوگ	Back *(adv.)*	Wāpas	واپس
Mad	Pāgal	پاگل	To alight	Utarnā	اُترنا

1. I am writing a letter to your father. 2. He is laughing like a mad man. 3. Who is this gentleman, who is coming towards us? 4. The train is still moving, do not alight. 5. Why are these men shouting here? 6. What were you doing in his room? 7. When we were coming back from the club, the women were going to the city. 8. The thieves were selling their things in the bazaar. 9. If the sick man is sleeping, do not awaken him. 10. My wife is giving some food to the poor people. 11. All the soldiers are cutting a large tree near the bridge. 12. All the friends are eating and drinking. 13. I was speaking to the girl whose father lives near my house. 14. Whom are you calling? 15. What! are you still sleeping? 16. Is my servant asleep or awake?

The Past Participle

The Past Participle is formed by adding "a" to the root, but if the root ends in "a" or "o", then "ya" is added; as,

			Root	Past Part.	
To speak	Bolnā	—	Bol	Bolā	بولا
To fly	Uṙnā	—	Uṙ	Uṙā	اُڑا
To drink	Pīnā	—	Pi	Pīā	پیا
To bring	Lānā	—	La	Lāyā	لایا
To sleep	Sona	—	So	Soyā	سویا

Exceptions:— *The following are the only Infinitives that take their Past Participles irregularly.*

			Masculine				Feminine			
			Singular		Plural		Singular		Plural	
To do	Karnā	—	Kīā	کیا	Kīē	کیے	Kī	کی	Kīṅ	کیں
To take	Lēnā	—	Līā	لیا	Līē	لیے	Lī	لی	Līṅ	لیں
To give	Dēnā	—	Dīā	دیا	Dīē	دیے	Dī	دی	Dīṅ	دیں
To be	Honā	—	Hūā	ہوا	Hūē	ہوئے	Hūī	ہوئی	Hūīṅ	ہوئیں
To go	Jānā	—	Gayā*	گیا	Gaē*	گئے	Gaī	گئی	Gaīṅ	گئیں

Note : — * Past Participles, formed by adding "ya" drop their "y" when "a" is changed into "e" or "i" for Gender and Number; as, He slept-Woh Soya, She slept-Woh soi. They slept-Woh soe.

Past Tense

(I, thou, he etc. walked)

Singular			Plural		
I walked	Maiṅ chalā	میں چلا	We walked	Ham chalē	ہم چلے
Thou walked	Tū chalā	تو چلا	You walked	Tum chalē	تم چلے
He walked	Woh chalā	وہ چلا	They walked	Woh chalē	وہ چلے
She walked	Woh chalī	وہ چلی	They walked (*f.*)	Woh chalīṅ	وہ چلیں

Past Perfect

Singular		
I have walked	Main chalā hūṅ	میں چلا ہوں
Thou hast walked	Tū chalā hai	تو چلا ہے
He has walked	Woh chalā hai	وہ چلا ہے
She has walked	Woh chalī hai	وہ چلی ہے

Plural		
We have walked	Ham chalē haiṅ	ہم چلے ہیں
You have walked	Tum chalē ho	تم چلے ہو
They have walked	Woh chalē haiṅ	وہ چلے ہیں
They have walked (*f.*)	Woh chalī haiṅ	وہ چلی ہیں
	Pluperfect	
Singular		
I had walked	Maiṅ chalā thā	میں چلا تھا
Thou hadst walked	Tū chalā thā	تو چلا تھا
He had walked	Woh chalā thā	وہ چلا تھا
She had walked	Woh chalī thī	وہ چلی تھی
Plural		
We had walked	Ham chalē thē	ہم چلے تھے
You had walked	Tum chalē thē	تم چلے تھے
They had walked	Woh chalē thē	وہ چلے تھے
They had walked (*f.*)	Woh chalī thīṅ	وہ چلی تھیں

Past Dubious Tense

The Past Dubious Tense is formed by adding the Future Tense of the Verb "to be" i.e., "hog ā" etc., to the Past Tense of a Verb: as,

Singular	Plural
I might have walked Maiṅ chalā hūṅgā. میں چلا ہوں گا	We might have walked. Ham chalē hoṅgē. ہم چلے ہوں گے

Singular	Plural
Thou might have walked. Tū chalā hogā. تو چلا ہوگا	You might have walked. Tum chalē hogē. or Ap chalē hoṅgē.
He might have walked. Woh chalā hogā. وہ چلا ہوگا	They might have walked. Woh chalē hoṅgē.
She might have walked. Woh chalī hogī. وہ چلی ہوگی	They (*f.*) might have walked. Woh chalī hoṅgī.

Examples

1. He brought my book from the office.
   (He, my book, office from, brought)—
   Woh mērī kitāb daftar sē lāyā.

2. My son has gone to your house.
   (My son, your house to, gone has [is])—
   Mērā bēṭā tumhārē ghar ko gayā hai.
   (or) Mērā bēṭā Āp kē ghar ko gayā hai.
3. The servants have fallen from the horses.
   (Servants, horses from, fallen have [are])—
   Naukar ghoṛoṅ sē girē haiṅ.

4. Your son had slept here.
   Your son, here, slept had, [was])—
   Tumhārā bēṭā yahāṅ soyā thā.

5. She did not come here yesterday.
   She, yesterday, here not (came)—
   Woh kal yahāṅ nahīṅ āī.

Exercise 22(a)

Guest	Mehmān	مہمان	Host	Mēzbān	میزبان
Merrily (*adv.*)	Khūshī sē	خوشی سے	Roof	Chhat	چھت

1. Hamārā ghořā Franklin sāheb kē pās kaun lēgayā hai? 2. Kal rāt ko maiň ghar kī chhat par soyā thā. 3. Āj tum daftar sē kitnē bajē wāpas āē? 4. Tumhārē sāheb kahāň gaē haīň? 5. Woh kal shām ko darzī kē pās gayā, aur mērē sab kapřē us sē lāyā. 6. Jab bach-cha jāgā, to uskī māň bahut haňsī, aur jaldī sē uskē pās āī. 7. Maiň nahīň jāntā hūň keh āj hamārā mehmān kīoň nahīň āyā. 8. Gharīb sāīs pichhlē mahīnē ghořē sē girā thā aur abhī tak tandurust nahīň hūā hai. 9. Jab mērī gāřī baňglē mēň pahuňchī, to mērī bīwī aur bach-chē gāřī kī ţaraf dauřē. 10. Maiň is ghořē par kabhī nahīň chařhā hūň. 11. Woh khūshī sē yeh khabar mērē pās lāē. 12. Jab ghar kī chhat girī to sab naukar bahut chil-lāē. 13. Bīmār ādmī palaňg par lēţā thā, aur uskē dost aur mēzbān uskē pās kursīoň par baiţhē thē.

Exercise 22(b)

India	Bhārat	بھارت	Joy	Khūshī	خوشی
Postman	Postman	پوسٹ مین	News	Khabar	خبر
	or Đākya	ڈاکیہ	Report	Khabar	خبر

1. Who has brought this letter? 2. The Postman has gone towards the mess. 3. When did you come here? 4. He never came to me. 5. How long did you wait there? 6. I have lived in India before. 7. We advanced and the enemy retreated. 8. The bridge has fallen into the river. 9. When did the Mail arrive? 10. We slept in the Dak bungalow. 11. The horse died last night. 12. Whose servant climbed (up) the tree? 13. When had the boys come here? 14. Whose keys had fallen there? 15. Who had gone to the College? 16. He stayed with me for three hours.

Past Tenses of Transitive Verbs

The foregoing rule deals with the Past Tenses of Intransitive Verbs only. The following is the rule for the Past Tenses of Transitive Verbs.

(a) The Particle "nē" (which has no proper translation in English, but can be regarded as equivalent to "by") is used after the subject of the following.

Past Tenses of the Transitive Verbs :—

1. Simple Past Perfect Tense; — I saw (Me by saw)
2. Past Perfect Tense;—I have seen (Me by seen is)
3. Pluperfect Tense; — I had seen (Me by seen was)
4. Past Dubious Tense; — I might have seen (Me by seen will be)

(b) When "nē" is used after the Subject, the Verb must agree in Gender and Number with the Object unless the latter is followed by a Post-Position.

(c) "Nē" like a Post-position inflects the Nouns, after which it is used.

EXAMPLES

1. The boy saw a horse (boy by a horse saw)—
Laṙkē nē ēk ghoṙā dēkhā. لڑکے نے ایک گھوڑا دیکھا

2. The man saw two horses (Man by two horses saw)—
Ādmī nē do ghoṙē dēkhē. آدمی نے دو گھوڑے دیکھے

3. The servant saw a mare (servant by a mare saw)—
Naukar nē ēk ghoṙī dēkhī. نوکر نے ایک گھوڑی دیکھی

4. The servants saw two mares.
(Servants by two mares saw)—
Naukaroṅ nē do ghoṙīāṅ dēkhiṅ. نوکروں نے دو گھوڑیاں دیکھیں

Conjugation

I saw Thou sawest He saw She saw	a horse	Maiň nē Tū nē Us nē Us nē	ēk ghořā dēkhā.
We saw You saw They saw	a horse	Ham nē Tum nē Unhoň nē	ēk ghořā dēkhā*

**As the Past Participle ends in "a", it is subject to change to agree in Number and Gender with the Object. Thus if the Object were "horses", "dēkhā" would become "dēkhē" : if a mare, "dēkhī"; if mares "dēkhīň". Similarly in the following tenses the Verb "honā" is made to agree in Gender and Number with the object.*

Past Perfect Tense

I have seen He has seen You have seen They have seen	a horse	Maiň nē Us nē Tum nē Unhon nē	ēk ghořā dēkhā hai**

*** "Dēkhā hai" becomes "dēkhē haiň" if horses; "dēkhī hai" if a mare; "dēkhī haiň" if mares.*

Pluperfect Tense

I had seen He had seen You had seen They had seen	a horse	Maiň nē Us nē Tum nē Unhoň nē	ēk ghořā dēkhā thā*

** "Dēkhā thā" would become "dēkhē thē" if horses; "dēkhī thī" if a mare; "dēkhī thīň" if mares.*

Past Dubious Tense

I might have seen He might have seen You might have seen They might have seen	a horse	Main nē Us nē Tum nē Unhoṅ nē	ēk ghoṙā dēkhā hogā**

** *"Dēkhā hogā" would become "dēkhē hoṅgē" if horses; "dēkhī hogī" if a mare; "dekhi hongi" if mares.*

Note:— If the Object of a Transitive Verb is some particular person or thing the Post-position "ko" is used after it to make it *definite*, and in that case the Verb remains unchanged. When the Object of a Transitive Verb is a human being whether definite, or not, it is always safe to use "ko" after it.

Examples

I have seen the mare	Maiṅ nē ghoṙī ko dēkhā hai.
They have seen the horses	Unhoṅ nē ghoṙoṅ ko dēkhā hai.
We saw the girl	Ham nē laṙkī ko dēkhā.
She saw the boys	Us nē laṙkoṅ ko dēkhā.

Exercise 23(a)

Girjā	Church	گرجا	Āfsar	Officer	افسر
Aisā	Such	ایسا	Pūlīs	Police	پولیس
Chēk	Cheque	چیک	To	Then	تو
Badmāsh	Wicked	بدمعاش	Pahlī dafa	First time	پہلی دفعہ

1. Ghūsl khānē kā darwāza kis nē kholā hai? 2. Jab dhobī kapṙē lāyā,

to naukar nē darwāza kholā aur kapřē sandūq mēň rakhē. 3. K͟hazānē kē afsar nē usko chēk kā rūpīa nahīň dīā. 4. Mērē bēṭē nē sab purānī kitābēň g͟harīb lařkē ko dīň 5. Us nē choroň ko dēkhā. 6. Maiň nahīň jāntā hūň kē us nē yeh chitthī mērē pās kīoň bhējī hai. 7. Maiň nē aisā tamāsha kabhī nahīň dēkhā hai. 8. Dhobī nē qasāī kē ghar kā tālā tořā. 9. Tum nē hamārē kapřē klub ko kīoň nahīň bhējē? 10. Is sipāhī nē pūlīs ko jhūṭī k͟habar bhējē. 11. Chār ādmīoň nē bahut sharāb pī, ēk dukān kē andar gaē, aur uskī sab khiřkīāň tořīň. 12. Bādshāh nē ēk bahut ach-chhā ghořā vazīr ko diā hai. 13. Ghoroň nē abhī tak dānā nahīň khāyā hai. 14. Badmāsh lařkoň nē ďāk gāřī par patthar phēňkē. 15. Maiň nahīň jāntā hūň keh us nē mērī jēb sē ghařī kab aur kaisē nikālī. 16. Maiň nē us lařkī ko pahlī dafa girjā mēň dēkhā thā.

Exercise 23(b)

Translate into English:—

۱۔ غسل خانہ کا دروازہ کس نے کھولا ہے۔ ۲۔ جب دھوبی کپڑے لایا تو نوکر نے دروازہ کھولا اور کپڑے صندوق میں رکھے۔ ۳۔ خزانے کے افسر نے اس کو چیک کا روپیہ نہیں دیا۔ ۴۔ میرے بیٹے نے سب پرانی کتابیں غریب لڑکے کو دیں۔ ۵۔ اس نے چوروں کو دیکھا۔ ۶۔ میں نہیں جانتا ہوں کہ اس نے یہ چھٹی میرے پاس کیوں بھیجی ہے۔ ۷۔ میں نے ایسا تماشہ کبھی نہیں دیکھا ہے۔ ۸ دھوبی نے قصائی کے گھر کا تالا توڑا۔ ۹ تم نے ہمارے کپڑے کلب کو کیوں نہیں بھیجے۔ ۱۰۔ اس سپاہی نے پولیس کو جھوٹی خبر بھیجی۔ ۱۱۔ چار آدمیوں نے بہت شراب پی، ایک دکان کے اندر گئے اور اس کی سب کھڑکیاں توڑ دیں۔ ۱۲۔ بادشاہ نے ایک بہت اچھا گھوڑا وزیر کو دیا ہے۔ ۱۳۔ گھوڑوں نے ابھی تک دانہ نہیں کھایا ہے۔ ۱۴۔ بدمعاش لڑکوں نے ڈاک گاڑی پر پتھر پھینکے۔ ۱۵۔ میں نہیں جانتا ہوں کہ اس نے میری جیب سے گھڑی کب اور کیسے نکالی۔ ۱۶۔ میں نے اس لڑکی کو پہلی مرتبہ گرجا میں دیکھا تھا۔

Exercise 23(c)

Cup	Pīāla	پیالہ	Monkey	Bandar	بندر
Garden	Bāgh	باغ	Shirt (*f.*)	Qamīz	قمیض
Telegram	Tār	تار	Permission (*f.*)	Ijāzat	اجازت
Washerman	Dhobī	دھوبی			

1. The servant opened the door. 2. She has broken two cups. 2. My son wrote a letter. 4. He has made two keys. 5. The girl has brought a lock. 6. He put the egg in my box. 7. What has this man done? 8. To whom did you give my letter? 9. I have brought two shirts from the tailor. 10. Where did you see my servant? 11. Who has made this table? 12. I might have seen the man. 13. My servants have burnt all the old letters of the office. 14. The washerman has changed my new shirt. 15. Did she show you the telegram? 16. When did you send that letter to me? 17. I did not call you. 18. He opened the letters without my permission. 19. Where did you put my watch last night? 20. The monkey broke all the windows of the shop. 21. I have never read such a good book before.

TRANSITIVE VERBS — (Continued)

It is very important to notice that some Verbs, which are Transitive in English, are treated as Intransitive in Urdu and, therefore, do not require the particle "nē" after the Subject in the Past Tense. They are as follows:—

To forget	Bhūlnā	بھولنا	To fight	Laṙnā	لڑنا
To bring	Lānā	لانا	To meet	Milnā	ملنا
To mount	Chaṙhnā	چڑھنا	To speak	Bolnā	بولنا
To reach	Pahuṅchnā	پہنچنا	To take away	Lējānā	لے جانا
To fear	Ḍarnā	ڈرنا	To finish	Chuknā	چکنا
				Khatam karnā	ختم کرنا

Examples

1. Our soldiers fought the battle bravely. Hamārē sipāhī laṙāī bahāduṙī sē laṙē.	ہمارے سپاہی لڑائی بہادری سے لڑے
2. He brought your horse to me. Woh tumhārā ghoṙā mērē pās lāyā.	وہ تمہارا گھوڑا میرے پاس لایا
3. He mounted the horse. Woh ghoṙē par chaṙhā.	وہ گھوڑے پر چڑھا

Past Conditional Tense

Conditional sentences are those in which one eventually is dependent on another. Past conditions are expressed in Urdu by using the present Participle, without any auxiliary Verb in both halves of the sentence, the first half being introduced by "agar" (if) and the second by "to" (then). The present Participles agree in Gender and Number with their respective Subjects.

If	the boy had come	then	the girl would have gone
agar	laṙkā ātā	to	laṙkī jātī

PAST CONDITIONAL TENSE (CONJUGATED)

Singular		
Had I seen	Agar maiṅ dēkhtā	اگر میں دیکھتا
Had thou seen	Agar tū dēkhtā	اگر تو دیکھتا
Had he seen	Agar who dēkhtā	اگر وہ دیکھتا
Had she seen	Agar woh dēkhtī	اگر وہ دیکھتی
Plural		
Had we seen	Agar ham dēkhtē	اگر ہم دیکھتے
Had you seen	Agar tum dēkhtē	اگر تم دیکھتے
Had they seen	Agar woh dēkhtē	اگر وہ دیکھتے
Had they seen (*f.*)	Agar woh dēkhtīṅ	اگر وہ دیکھتیں

THEN		
I would have gone	To maiṅ jātā	تو میں جاتا
Thou would have gone	To tū jātā	تو تو جاتا
He would have gone	To woh jātā	تو وہ جاتا
She would have gone	To who jātī	تو وہ جاتی
THEN		
We would have gone	To ham jātē	تو ہم جاتے
You would have gone	To tum jātē	تو تم جاتے
They would have gone	To woh jātē	تو وہ جاتے
They would have gone (*f.*)	To woh jātīṅ	تو وہ جاتیں

EXAMPLES

1. If you had slept here, (then) I would have awakened you.
   Āgar tum yahāṅ sotē, to maīṅ tum ko jagātā.

2. If he had sent for me, I would have come.
   Āgar woh mujh ko bulātā, to maīṅ atā.

3. If you had brought the cloth, I would have bought it.
   Āgar tum kapṙā lātē, to maīṅ <u>kh</u>arīdtā.

4. Had they come here, she would have waited.
   Āgar woh yahāṅ ātē, to woh ţhairtī.

5. Had the girls seen you, they would have laughed.
   Āgar laṙkiīāṅ tum ko dēkhtīṅ, to woh haṅstīṅ.

Note:— Instead of "would have", "might have" is used in English to show doubt or uncertainly, and "must have" to denote certainty. The construction in Urdu is the same, except that words "sh āyad" (perhaps) and "zar ūr" (certainly) are inserted respectively in the second sentence; as,

1. If they had taken the boy to a doctor, he might not have died.
   Āgar woh lar̄kē ko d̄ākṭār sāheb kē pās lējātē, to shāyad woh nahīň martā.

2. If my son had seen you, he must have called you.
   Āgar mērā bēṭā tum ko dēkhtā, to woh tum ko zarūr bulātā.

EXERCISE 24(A)

Dāna	Grain	دانہ	Chokar (*f.*)	Bran	چوکر
Jaňgal	Jungle	جنگل	Jaňglī	Wild	جنگلی
Āg (*f.*)	Fire	آگ	D̄āk gār̄ī	Mail Train	ڈاک گاڑی
D̄āk	Mail	ڈاک			

1. Agar maiň daftar ko jātā, to tumhārē wāstē bāzaār sē kāghaz lātā. 2. Agar āp yeh chit-thī mērē bēṭē kē pās lējātē, to woh āpkē sāth jātā. 3. Agar chor mērē baňglē kē andar ātā, to kuttā uskē pīchhē daur̄tā. 4. Agar tum rāt ko jaňgal mēň āg jalātē, to shēr aur sab jaňglī jānwar bhāgtē. 5. Agar who bandūq bēchtā, to maiň usko do sau rupai dētā. 6. Agar mērā naukar dānā yā chokar churātā, to maiň usko pūlīs mēň bhējtā. 7. Agar mērē naukar kē bach-chē rāt ko chil-lātē, to maiň unko bahut mārtā. 8. Agar daftar kē ādmi tum ko jāntē, to woh tum ko mērī d̄āk zarūr dētē. 9. Agar uskī bēṭī yeh khabar suntī, to woh bahut rotī. 10. Agar woh auratēň mērī dukān ko ātīň, to shāyad bahut chīzēň kharīdtīň. 11. Agar woh d̄āk gār̄ī sē bhī ātē, to bhī abhī tak yahāň nahīň pahuňchtē.

EXERCISE 24(B)

Reward	Inām	انعام	Recommendation	Sifārish	سفارش
To steal	Churānā	چُرانا	Receipt	Rasīd	رسید
Engineer	Injīnyar	انجینیر	Guard	Gārd	گارڈ

1. If he had sold the horse, my son would have bought it. 2. If you had gone to the office, you would have seen me. 3. If he knew it, I would not have sent the letter. 4. Had the boy seen the watch, he would have given it to me. 5. Had I borken the cup, I would have told you. 6. Had these men come to me, I might have given them work. 7. Had the engineer seen you here, he would have called you. 8. Had the postmaster given me any receipt, I must have brought it to you. 9. If the girls had gone to the school, the women must have seen them. 10. If you had told the guard, he might have awakened you.

The Aorist Tense

The Aorist Tense (e.g., I may go, he may come, etc.) is formed by adding, to the root of the Verb, the following endings for the different Persons:—

Singular			Plural		
I	(takes)	Root + ūň	We	(takes)	Root + ēň
Thou	”	Root + ē	You	”	Root + o
He & She	”	Root + ē	They	”	Root + ēň

Aorist Tense (Conjugated)

I may go	Maiň jāūň	میں جاؤں	We may go	Ham jāēň	ہم جائیں
Thou may go	Tū jāē	تو جائے	You may go	Tum jāo	تم جاؤ
He may go She may go	Woh jāē	وہ جائے	They may go	Woh jāēň	وہ جائیں

Note:— (a) When "may" denotes doubt or uncertainty the word "shāyad" (perhaps) is inserted in the sentence; as:

1. I may write a letter to him.
   Shāyad maiň us ko ēk <u>kh</u>at likhūň. شاید میں اس کو ایک خط لکھوں

2. My servant may bring the horse.
Shāyad mērā naukar ghoṙā lāē. شاید میرا نوکر گھوڑا لائے

3. We may go there today.
Shāyad ham āj wahāṅ jāēṅ. شاید ہم آج وہاں جائیں

4. You may see him in the office.
Shāyad tum usko daftar mēṅ dēkho. شاید تم اس کو دفتر میں دیکھو

5. They may not arrive here by ten.
Shāyad woh das bajē tak yahāṅ nahīṅ pahuṅchēṅ.
شاید وہ دس بجے تک یہاں نہیں پہونچیں

Note:— (b) The Aorist Tense is employed in Urdu, when the Present Indefinite Tense occurs in English after "if", "when" and "until" and the Verb of the second clause is in the Imperative; as will be seen from the following examples.

6. If he comes here, give him this letter.
Agar woh yahāṅ āē (not "ātā hai"), to yeh chiṭ-ṭhī usko do.

7. When I go there, show me the carriage.
Jab maiṅ wahāṅ jāūṅ to mujh ko gāṙī dikhāo.

8. If he laughs again, turn him out.
Agar woh phir haṅsē, to usko nikālo.

EXERCISE 25(A)

Itwar	Sunday	اتوار	Kishti	Boat	کشتی

1. Shāyad maiṅ aglē itwār ko girjā jāūṅ. 2. Shāyad āj sham ko woh bāgh mēṅ āē. 3. Shāyad aglē mahīṅē mēṅ ham tum ko do qamīsēṅ dēṅ. 4. Shāyad dushman āj rāt ko pul toṙē 5. Shāyad dākya hamārī chiṭ-thīāṅ daftar ko lējāē. 6. Shāyad hamārē mehmān āj hoṭal mēṅ Khānā Khāēṅ. 7. Shāyad mērā naukar ḍāk gāṙī sē āē. 8. Shāyad woh badmāsh ādmī yeh sandūq rāstē mēṅ kholēṅ. 9. Agar daryā mēṅ bahut pānī ho, to shāyad ham kishtīoṅ mēṅ

jāēn̐. 10. Agar darzī hamārē kapṛē lāē to sandūq kē andar mat rakho. 11. Agar yeh ādmī ṭhīk kām nahīn̐ karē, to is ko manījar sāheb kē pās lējāo. 12. Jab editor sāheb daftar mēn̐ āēn̐, to mujh ko khabar do. 13. Jab tak ham wāpas na āēn̐, tum yahān̐ ṭhairo. 14. Agar chaukīdār rāt ko soē, to usko fauran jagāo.

EXERCISE 25(B)

To obey	Mānnā	ماننا	Syce	Sāīs	سائیس
To remind	Yād dilānā	یاد دلانا	Pay	Tankhwāh	تنخواہ

1. I may bring it back tomorrow. 2. He may send you pay from Bombay. 3. We may not cut this tree today. 4. You may not go there tomorrow. 5. They may go across the river in boats. 6. He may not buy your horse. 7. Remind it to me, when I come here tomorrow. 8. If the driver brings my car, send him to my office. 9. When they go to the mess, show them this horse. 10. If he does not obey your order, bring him to me. 11. Wake me up at once, if any one brings a letter for me. 12. If the women come here, send them to the club.

The Future Tense

The Future Tense is formed by adding to the root of a Verb the following terminations for the different Persons;

Singular					Plural			
I	(takes)	Root	+	ūn̐gā	We	Root	+	ēn̐gē
Thou	"	"	+	ēgā	You	"	+	ogē
He	"	"	+	ēgā	They	"	+	ēn̐gē
She	"	"	+	ēgī	They (*f.*)	"	+	ēn̐gī

Future Tense — *Conjugated*			
I shall go	Main jāūṅgā	We shall go	Ham jāēṅgē
Thou shalt go	Tu jāēgā	You will go	Tum jāogē
He will go	Woh jāēgā	They will go	Woh jāēṅgē
She will go	Woh jāēgī	They will go (*f.*)	Woh jāēṅgī

EXAMPLES

1. I shall write a letter.
   Maiṅ ēk chiṭ-ṭhī likhūṅgā. میں ایک چٹھی لکھوں گا
2. His servant will not open your box.
   Uskā naukar tumhārā sandūq nahīṅ kholēgā. اس کا نوکر تمہارا صندوق نہیں کھولے گا
3. We shall send you there.
   Ham tum ko wahāṅ bhējēṅgē. ہم تم کو وہاں بھیجیں گے
4. When will you reach Delhi?
   Tum Dehlī kab pahuṅchogē? تم دہلی کب پہنچو گے ؟
5. Will these men sit in this room?
   Kiā yeh ādmī is kamre meṅ baiṭhenge? کیا یہ آدمی اِس کمرے میں بیٹھیں گے ؟
6. The mare will not eat this bad grass.
   Ghoṛī yeh <u>kh</u>arāb ghāṅs nahīṅ khāēgī. گھوڑی یہ خراب گھاس نہیں کھائے گی
7. His daughters will come here this evening.
   Uskī bēṭīāṅ āj shām ko yahāṅ āēṅgī. اُس کی بیٹیاں آج شام کو یہاں آئیں گی

EXERCISE 26(A)

Qasūr	Fault	قصور	Hāth	Hand	ہاتھ
Pahār	Hill	پہاڑ	Qulī	Coolie	قلی
Fauj	Army	فوج	Faujī; Sipāhī	Soldier	فوجی

1. Tum āj daftar ko kīoñ nahīñ jāogē? 2. Woh shikār sē kab wāpas āēgā? 3. Agar yeh tumhārā qasūr nahīñ hai, to woh tum ko sazā nahīñ dēgā. 4. Do sau faujī kal subah pahāṛ ko jāēñgē. 5. Un kē sāth kaun jāēgā. 6. Āj hamārē naukar hamārā kamra sāf karēñgē. 7. Agar tum aisā qasūr phir karogē, to woh tum ko bahut mārēgā. 8. Agar tum sīpahīoñ kē hāth phir sharāb bēchogē, to ham tum ko pūlīs mēñ bhējēñgē. 9. Shāyad ḍāk gāṛī shām ko pāñch bajē yahāñ pahuñchēgī. 10. Tum kal sawērē kitnē bajē uṭhogē? 11. Qulī saṛak kab tak taī-yār karēñgē? 12. Laṛkīāñ aur auratēñ āj rāt ko das bajē yahāñ pahuñchēñgī.

EXERCISE 26(B)

Shooting	Shikār	شکار	Advance	Pēshgī	پیشگی
Dance	Nāch	ناچ	Mistake	Ghalti	غلطی
Lame	Lañgṛā	لنگڑا	Race (Horse)	Ghuṛdauṛ	گھڑدوڑ

1. I shall not go to the club today. 2. Will your brother read this book? 3. When will the coolies arrive here? 4. I shall send two servants with you. 5. The Major will not come to the office today. 6. Who will give you two hundred rupees for this lame horse? 7. He will not give you any advance. 8. I shall be ready presently. 9. I know that you will not make such a mistake again. 10. Will you also go with my brother for shooting? 11. His wife will not go with him to the dance. 12. Two mares will also run in the race. 13. I will beat your son, if I see him again in this room.

REVISIONAL EXERCISE 27

(On Exercises from 22 to 28)

Owner	Mālik	مالک	Holiday *f.*	Chhuṭ-ṭi	چھٹی
Fruit	Mēwa, phal	میوہ/پھل	Bottle *f.*	Botal	بوتل
Case (state)	Hāl	حال	To spend	Kharch karnā	خرچ کرنا

Ripe, mature	Pakkā	پکا	To look for	Talāsh karnā	تلاش کرنا
To think	Sochnā	سوچنا	To explain	Samjhānā	سمجھانا
Ago	Hūā; hūē (*pb.*) ہوا، ہوئے		During	Mēň; kē arsē meň میں ، کے عرصے میں	

1. The ripest fruit falls first (of all). 2. Whom are you calling? 3. I do not eat meat often. 4. I am looking for my hat, which I put on this table an hour ago. 5. Why have you not got up yet? 6. What were you doing with that knife? 7. Do you not see what I am doing? 8. Who is this gentleman, who is coming towards us? 9. Where is the envelope on which you wrote the address just now? 10. I am going home, will you come with me? 11. What did you do during the holidays? 12. Somebody is calling you. 13. This is not the stick, which I left in that corner; some one has changed it. 14. If you had told the waiter, he would have brought two bottles of beer, one for you and one for me. 15. I do not know why he has not sent the reply to my letter yet. 16. If you see the dog in the garden, send it back to its owner. 17. If the doctor had come here, I would have shown him the wound. 18. I have heard that he will not do it. 19. If I had given even one hundred rupees to my servant, he would have spent them all in one day. 20. What are you thinking about? 21. I heard all what he said. 22. He may not arrive here by ten. 23. I will give the children all the fruits and flowers, which I brought from the jungle.

The Past Conjunctive

It often happens in English that two or more Verbs are joined together by the Conjunction "and". In such cases, to implify the construction, the word "and" is omitted and its place is taken by the Conjunctive Participle. This is formed by adding "kar" to the root of Verbs; as,

Having seen	Dēkh kar دیکھ کر	Having opened	Khol kar کھول کر
Go and see	Jā kar dēkho. جا کر دیکھو	Come and play	Ā kar khēlo. آ کر کھیلو

1. He opened the door and came in.
   Woh darwāza khol kar andar āyā.

2. I shall go there, and see him,
   Maiṅ wahāṅ jākar usko dēkhūṅgā.

3. He laughed and said.
   Us nē haṅs kar kahā.

EXERCISE 28(A)

Farsh	Floor	فرش	Ghāṅs	Grass	گھانس
Hiran	Buck	ہرن	Mehrbānī sē	Please	مہربانی سے

1. Yeh chiṭ-ṭhī Baṅk ko dēkar bāzār ko jāo. 2. Yeh chiṭ-ṭhī paṙh kar mehrbānī sē iskā jawāb jaldī do. 3. Kamrē sē sab chīzēṅ bāhar nikal kar farsh aur dīwārēṅ sāf karo. 4. Sāis ghoṙē ko dāna dē kar ghāṅs kē wāstē bāzaār gayā hai. 5. Ham nē ḍāk baṅglē mēṅ jā kar khānā khāyā. 6. Samī sāheb nē usko tankhwah dē kar baṅglē sē nikālā. 7. Sab laṙkīāṅ ach-chhē kapṙē pahen kar nāch mēṅ jāēṅgī. 8. Ék faujī nē apnē kapṙē bēch kar sharāb pī. 9. Tum khānā khā kar jaldī wāpas āo. 10. Maiṅ Karāchī jā kar ēk motor kharīdūṅgā. 11. Mērī bīwī Queṭṭa pahuṅch kar mujh ko khat likhēgī. 12. Hamārē sipāhīoṅ nē darakht kāt kar pul banāyā. 13. Hiran shēr ko dēkh kar bhāgā. 14. Woh bīmār ho kar pahār ko gayā hai.

EXERCISE 28(B)

Pillow	Takya	تکیہ	Basket	Tokrī	ٹوکری
To hide	Chhupanā	چھپانا	To rub	Malnā	ملنا
Newspaper	Akhbār	اخبار	Bicycle	Bysikal	بائیسکل

1. Come here, and take off my boots. 2. The monkey took off his

turban, and climbed up a tree. 3. Take off the saddle, and rub the horse well. 4. Put these things in a basket, and send them to my bungalow. 5. Run after him, and call him back. 6. Go to the mess, and bring some cord from Ābdar. 7. My brother will read the newspaper and then give it to you. 8. He stopped the carriage, and gave a rupee to the old man. 9. My servant broke my watch, and hid it under my pillow. 10. Will you sell the horse, and buy a bicycle? 11. He stole my razors, and sold them in the bazaar.

Use of "apnā" اپنا

When a Possessive Pronoun, of whatever person or Number (such as my, our, thy, your, his, their, her, or its, etc.) refers to the Subject of the sentence, and occurs in the same sub-clause as the Subject, it is always translated by "apnā".

EXAMPLES

1. I was reading my book.
   Maiṅ apnī kitāb paṛh rahā thā. — میں اپنی کتاب پڑھ رہا تھا

2. They were coming from their office.
   Woh apnē daftar sē ā rahē thē. — وہ اپنے دفتر سے آ رہے تھے

3. Will you write a letter to your father?
   Tum apnē bāp ko khat likhogē? — تم اپنے باپ کو خط لکھو گے

4. The girl will take her dog with her.
   Laṛkī apnā kuttā apnē sāth lējāēgī. — لڑکی اپنا کتا اپنے ساتھ لے جائے گی

Note (i) :— In the case of command or the Imperative Mood, (when the Second Personal Pronoun "you" is, as a rule, omitted or understood), if "your" is used; it must be translated by "apnā"; as,

1. Bring your book — Apni kitāb lāo. — اپنی کتاب لاؤ
2. Open your box — Apnā sandūq kholo. — اپنا صندوق کھولو

3. Take this letter with you to the Secretary.
 Yeh chiṭ-thī apnē sāth Secreṭary sāheb kē pās lējāo.

 یہ چٹھی اپنے ساتھ سکریٹری صاحب کے پاس لے جاؤ

Note (2) : — If a Conjunction or a Relative Pronoun is used between the subject of the sentence and the Possessive Pronoun referring to it, the use of "apna" is inadm īssible.

1. I and my son will go there.
 Maiṅ aur mērā (not apnā) bēṭā wahāṅ jāēṅge. میں اور میرا بیٹا وہاں جائیں گے
2. I shall read my book, which is on my table.
 Maiṅ apnī kitāb paṙhūṅgā, jo mērī mēz per hai.

 میں اپنی کتاب پڑھوں گا۔ جو میری میز پر ہے

Note (3) :— "Apna" is also used as a Reflexive Pronoun to translate the English "myself", "yourself", "himself", etc. as,

1. He found himself in a trap.
 Us nē apnē ko ēk jāl mēṅ pāyā. اس نے اپنے کو ایک جال میں پایا
2. You have ruined yourself.
 Tum nē apnē ko barbād kīā hai. تم نے اپنے کو برباد کیا ہے

EXERCISE 29(A)

Parda	Curtain	پردہ	Izzat	Honour	عزّت

1. Mujh ko apnī chiṭ-ṭhīāṅ dikhāo. 2. Apnē sāheb ko hamārā salām do. 3. Apnē kapṙē badal kar mērē pās āo. 4. Mērā naukar chiṭ-ṭhī lē kar apnē ghar ko gayā hai. 5. Gharīb ādmī apnī sab chīzēṅ bēchēgā. 6. Tum apnī dukāṇ kīoṅ nahīṅ kholtē ho? 7. Apnā palaṅg barāmdē mēṅ mat rakho. 8. Sipāhī apnī bandūq apnē sandūq mēṅ nahīṅ rakhtā hai. 9. Qureshī sāheb nē apnē naukar ko das rupai dē kar usko pahāṙ bhējā. 10. Kuchh log apnī aurtoṅ ko pardē mēṅ rakhtē haiṅ. 11. Tum apnī sab chīzēṅ lē kar hamārē

baṅglē sē fauran bāhar jāo. 12. Jab aurat nē apnā bach-chā palaṅg per nahīṅ dēkhā to woh bahut roī. 13. Maiṅ apnē bāp sē pūchh kar tum ko jawāb dūṅgī. 14. Maiṅ apnī ghaṙī apnē sandūq mēṅ rakh kar daftaṙ ko gayā thā. 15. Apnī izzat apnē hāth hai.

EXERCISE 29(B)

Lesson	Sabaq	سبق	Eye (f.)	Āṅkh	آنکھ
Wound	Za<u>kh</u>m	زخم	To Waste	Zāē karnā	ضائع کرنا
Wounded	Za<u>kh</u>mī	زخمی	Dacoit	Ḍākū	ڈاکو
Mouth	Mūṅh	منہ	Well	Kūāṅ	کنواں
Tent	Ḍera; <u>Kh</u>ēma ڈیرہ / خیمہ		To disgrace	Ruswā karnā	رسوا کرنا

1. Clean your hands, and change your clothes. 2. Open your book, and read your lesson. 3. He took off his hat, and showed me his wound. 4. You never keep your hands clean. 5. I will give you two rupees from my own pocket. 6. Shut your mouth and open your eyes. 7. When the dacoits arrived, the people ran out of their houses. 8. I shall take my servant with me. 9. My servant will go to his house next week. 10. The poor man was sitting in his shop. 11. Why do you waste your time? 12. The saheb has killed a thief, who was in his tent last night. 13. He and his horse fell into a deep well. 14. Will you see the man who has brought your horse? 15. She will disgrace herself.

Use of "Āp" آپ

The word "āp" is employed to lay emphasis on the subject of a sentence in the same way that "myself", "yourself", "himself", are used in English. This construction must not be confused with the reflexive apna" which also translates "myself" etc. though with a different meaning (vide *Note* 3 page 104).

EXAMPLES

1. I will go their myself.
   Maiň āp wahāň jāūňgā.

2. My servant came here himself.
   Mērā naukar āp yahāň āyā.

3. She has written this letter herself.
   Us nē āp yeh chiţ-ţhī līkhī hai.

4. Will you yourself live in this room?
   Kiā tum āp is kamrē mēň rahogē?

5. The soldiers themselves will make the bridge.
   Sipāhī āp pul banāēňgē?

EXERCISE 30(A)

1. Lařkē nē āp apnī ghařī tořī hai. 2. Ham āp uskī dūkān ko jāēňgē. 3. Gharīb auratēň apnē ghar kā kām āp kartī haiň. 4. Yeh chiţ-ţhī maiň āp Khān Sāheb kē pās lējāūňgā. 5. Mērā saīs āp ghořē kē wāstē ghāňs nahīň lāēgā. 6. Mērē bach-chē āp yeh kitābēň pařhēňgē. 7. Dhobī kā bēţā āp hamārī qamīs taī-yār karēgā. 8. Yeh lifāfa tum mat kholo, maiň āp kholūňgā. 9. Faujī log āp rāsta sāf karēňgē. 10. Maulvī sāheb nē āp tum ko bāgh mēň dēkhā thā. 11. Darzī āp kā kām nahīň kartā hai. 12. Sab naukar apnē kapřē āp kharīdēňgē. 13. Tum āp qasāī kē pās jāo, aur usko mērē pās lāo.

EXERCISE 30(B)

Address	Pata	پتہ	To drive	Chalānā	چلانا
On foot	Paidal	پیدل	Brave	Bahādur	بہادر

1. I am going that way myself. 2. The king himself will give a reward to his brave soldiers. 3. If the tailor does not come here himself, I will not

give him any work in future. 4. The woman herself was on the horse, and her husband was on foot. 5. Did you yourself see him there? 6. Take this letter to the post office yourself. 7. He did not give me his address himself. 8. He will open his letter himself. 9. She will make the tea herself. 10. Will you come to me yourself? 11. The Saheb will drive his motor himself.

The Days of the Week

English	Urdu		English	Urdu	
Sunday	Itwār	اتوار	Thursday	Jumērāt	جمعرات
Monday	Pīr	پیر	Friday	Jumā	جمعہ
Tuesday	Mañgal	منگل	Saturday	Hafta	ہفتہ / سنیچر
Wednesday	Budh	بدھ			

N.B. — Days of the week always take 'ko' after them; as, on Sunday — Itwār ko (not Itwār par)

Directions

English	Urdu	اردو	English	Urdu	اردو
North	Shimal	شمال	East	Mashriq	مشرق
South	Janūb	جنوب	West	Maghrib	مغرب

The Verbal Noun

In English the Infinitive and the Present Participle of a Verb are often used as Noun. In Urdu the Infinitive is employed in the same way and is subject to inflection when governed by a Post-position.

EXAMPLES

Nominative

1. Rising early is very good.
Sawērē uṭhnā bahut ach-chhā hai. سویرے اٹھنا بہت اچھا ہے

Nominative

2. It is very bad to tell a lie.
Jhūt bolnā bahut kharāb hai. جھوٹ بولنا بہت برا ہے

Objective

1. He is fond of eating.
Woh khānē kā shauqīn hai. وہ کھانے کا شوقین ہے

2. The glass was broken in coming.
Shīsha ānē mēň tūt gayā. شیشہ آنے میں ٹوٹ گیا

3. It does not cost anything to be polite.
Mīthā bolnē mēň kuchh kharch nahīň hotā hai. میٹھا بولنے میں کچھ خرچ نہیں ہوتا ہے

EXERCISE 31(A)

Jurm	Crime	جرم	Rishwat *f.*	Bribe	رشوت
Farq	Difference	فرق	Gālī	Abuse	گالی
Dāňt	Tooth	دانت	Dunyā *f.*	World	دنیا
Bachānā	To save	بچانا	Gānā	To sing	گانا
Kamānā	To earn	کمانا	Hūshyār	Clever	ہوشیار
Tārīf karnā	To praise	تعریف کرنا	Lēnē dēnē mēň	In dealing	لینے دینے میں

1. Tum tairnā jāntē ho? 2. Mērī bīwī haňsnā nahīň jāntī hai. 3. Rishwat lēnā aur dēnā donoň jurm haiň. 4. Sust ādmī sirf khānā khānā aur khānē kē bād sonā pasand kartē haiň. 5. Dunyā mēň gānā aur ronā kaun nahīň jāntā hai. 6. Kabhī kabhī tārīf karnā gālī dēnē sē kharāb hai. 7. Thořī dēr khēlnā band karo, aur thořā kām karo. 8. Karnē aur kehnē mēň bahut farq hai. 9. Yeh bud-dhā ādmī jhūṭ bolnē mēň bahut hūshyār hai. 10. Paisa bachānā paisa kamānē kē barābar hai. 11. Bahādur ādmī marnē aur mārnē sē nahīň ḍartē haiň. 12. Dūsroň kī jēb sē paise nikālnā āsān nahīň hai. 13. Woh ādmī lēnē dēnē mēň thīk nahīň hai. 14. Har waqt haňsnā aur dāňt nikālnā bahut kharāb ādatēň haiň. 15. Āgē bařhnē mēň kiā mushkilēň thīň? 16. Bāt banānā āsān hai, lēkin kām karnā muskhil hai.

EXERCISE 31(B)

Rest	Ārām	آرام	Occupation	Shughl	شغل
Debt	Qarz	قرض	Favourite	Dil pasand	دل پسند
Healthy	Tandrust	تندرست	Wealthy	Daulatmand	دولتمند
Sign	Ishāra	اشارہ	Method	Tarīqa	طریقہ
Excuse	Uzr	عذر	To be silent	Chup rahnā	چپ رہنا
Habit *f.*	Ādat	عادت	Language *f.*	Zabān	زبان
To like	Pasand karnā	پسند کرنا	To talk	Bāt karnā	بات کرنا
To smoke	Huqqa pīnā	حقہ پینا	To lend	Qarz dēnā	قرض دینا
To borrow	Qarz lēnā	قرض لینا	To learn	Sīkhnā	سیکھنا
To leave off	Chhoṙnā	چھوڑنا	To bite	Kāṭnā	کاٹنا
To smoke a cigareet	Sigrīṭ pīnā	سگریٹ پینا	Kitchen	Bāwarchī khāna	باورچی خانہ
To start	Rawāna honā	روانہ ہونا	To begin	shrū karnā	شورکرنا

1. My servant does not like working. 2. His favourite occupation is talking and smoking behind the kitchen. 3. That was the sign for starting. 4. Lending and brrowing are both bad habits. 5. What is the best method of learning a language? 6. Leave off writing for a short time, and take a little rest. 7. To make an excuse is worse than the fault itself. 8. Their bark is worse than their bite. 9. Early to bed, and early to rise makes a man healthy, wealthy and wise. 10. It is better to be silent than to speak in anger.

Infinitive of Purpose

In Urdu, as in English, the Infinitive is used to express purpose or intention. In such cases the inflected form of the Infinitive, followed by "ko" is employed. "Ko" may be omitted when the Verb, preceding the Infinitive, is a Verb of motion specially "ānā" and "j ānā". It will, however, be safer to use "ko" always.

EXAMPLES

1. I sat down under a tree *to take* rest.
   Maiṅ ārām lēnē (ko) ēk dara<u>kh</u>at kē nīchē baiṭhā.

2. My brother has gone *to play* polo.
   Mērā bhāī polo khēlnē (ko) gayā hai.

3. He has come *to take* his pay.
   Woh apnī tan<u>kh</u>wāh lēnē (ko) āyā hai.

EXERCISE 32(A)

<u>Kh</u>udā	God	خدا	Pat-thar	Stone	پتھر
Jāsūs	Spy	جاسوس	Miṭhāī *f.*	Sweetmeat	مٹھائی
Tār	Wire	تار	Naukar rakhnā	To employ	نوکر رکھنا

1. Maiṅ abhī huqqa pīnē ko gayā thā. 2. Woh mērē pās das rupai qarz lēnē ko āyā 3. Ūskē bēṭē moṭor chalānā sīkhnē ko Lahorē gaē haiṅ. 4. Jāsūs ṭēlīfūn kā tār kāṭnē ko dra<u>kh</u>t par chaṙhā. 5. Tum uskē kamrē mēṅ kiā karnē gaē thē? 6. <u>Kh</u>udā nē din kām karnē ko aur rāt ārām karnē ko banāī hai. 7. Maiṅ āp ko salām karnē āyā hūṅ. 8. Mērā bhāī āj shām khānā khānē ko yahāṅ āēgā. 9. Woh sab log tamāsha dēkhnē jāēṅgē. 10. Chor uskē sandūq kā tālā toṙnē ko ēk baṙā pat-thar lāē. 11. Pichhlē mahīnē mērī bahnen mujh ko dēkhnē ko āīṅ. 12. Tum uskē pās kīā pūchhnē ko gāē thē. 13. Maiṅ ne tum ko tumhārā mūṅh dēkhnē ko naukar nahīṅ rakhā hai. 14. Tumhārā naukar tum ko bulānē āyā hai. 15. Maiṅ tumhārē pās baiṭhnē ko nahīṅ āyā hūṅ. 16. Tum yahāṅ sīkhnē ko āē ho keh (or yā) sikhānē? 17. Yeh do rupai tumhārē miṭhāī khānē ko haiṅ.

EXERCISE 32(B)

Goat	Bakrā	بکرا	She-goat	Bakrī	بکری
To stop	Roknā	روکنا	To pull	Khēňchnā	کھینچنا
Watch-maker	Gharī sāz	گھڑی ساز	Sweeper	Mehtar	مہتر
To attack	Hamla karnā	حملہ کرنا	To think	Khīyāl karnā	خیال کرنا
Crowd	Hujūm; Bhīř	ہجوم / بھیڑ	Collector	Kalakṭar sāheb	کلکٹر صاحب
To distribute	Taqsīm karnā or Bāňṭnā	تقسیم کرنا / بانٹنا	Head Master	Head Masṭer sāheb	ہیڈ ماسٹر صاحب
To live (to exist)	Jīnā	جینا	To live (to dwell)	Rahnā	رہنا

1. The tiger came to eat the goat. 2. We do not live to eat, but we eat to live. 3. He will come here to live in this bungalow for two months. 4. My servant came to light the lamp. 5. The manager of the hotel came himself to change the sheet of my bed. 6. The gentleman has come here to learn Urdu. 7. I will give you ten rupees to buy woollen clothes. 8. I do not pay you to break my things. 9. The sweeper will go to Lahore to bring the dogs. 10. I went to see the Collector yesterday. 11. I think you have come here to humbug me. 12. The tailor came to show me the cloth. 13. He went inside to make the beds. 14. The boy has gone to help the wounded. 15. I sent my servant to call a watch-maker. 16. Didn't anybody call to see me? 17. The Police soon arrived to disperse the crowd. 18. The thief took out a knife to attack (upon) me, but I pulled the chain to stop the train. 19. The Head Master gave me ten rupees to buy sweets to distribute among the children.

The Passive Voice

We have seen that the English construction "I have walked" becomes in Urdu, "I am walked." Similarly the English "I am beaten" becomes in Urdu, "go beaten." The latter is called the Passive Voice.

In Urdu, as well as in English, the Passive construction is complicated by the fact that the Object of the action is in the Nominative Form; as, The body was seen, The spy was shot. He was sent ahead.

Here although "Boy," "Spy" and "He" are all in the Nominative, they do not act, but are acted upon. In such cases the Passive Voice of the Verb is used.

The passive Voice is, of course, restricted to Transitive Verbs and is formed by adding "jānā" (to go) to the Past Participle, as:—

To be seen	Dēkhā jānā	دیکھا جانا	To be brought	Lāyā jānā	لایا جانا

Note :— Both the Past Participle and the Auxiliary Verb "jānā" are inflected, so as to agree with the Noun, which is acted upon.

EXAMPLES

1. The box is opened.	Sandūq kholā jātā hai.
2. The eggs are sold	Andē bēchē jātē haiṅ.
3. The girl had been seen.	Laṙkī dēkhī gaī thī.
4. The lock will be broken	Tālā toṙā jāēgā.
5. The clothes have been brought	Kapṙē lāē gaē haiṅ.
6. The mares will be bought.	Ghoṙīāṅ Kharīdī jāēṅgī.

EXERCISE 33(A)

Laṙāī	Battle; war	لڑائی	Arzī	Petition	عرضی
Palṭan	Regiment	پلٹن	Jēl	Jail	جیل

1. Yeh hukm sab palṭanoṅ ko bhējā gayā thā. 2. Tum ko sab chīzēṅ dikhāī gaī thīṅ. 3. Bahādur sipāhī jo laṙāī mēṅ mārā gayā hai, abhī jawān

thā, aur uskī bīwī ko baṛā inām dīā jāēgā. 4. Sab kamzor aur bīmār sipāhī aglē mahīnē mēṅ pahāṛ ko bhējē jāēṅgē. 5. Dushman kā hawāī jahāz girāyā gayā. 6. Agar tum baṅglē kē pās phir dēkhē jaogē, to jēl ko bhējē jāogē. 7. Sab sipāhī chhuṭ-ṭī sē wāpas bulāē gaē haiṅ. 8. Ab yeh hukm likhā gayā hai, ab badlā nahīṅ jāēgā. 9. Hamārī chiṭ-ṭhī kis kē sāmnē kholī gaī thī? 10. Tumhārī arzī Jaj Sāheb kē sāmnē rakhī jāēgī.

EXERCISE 33(B)

Waste paper	Raddī kāghaz	ردّی کاغذ	To make noise	Shor karnā	شور کرنا
Effects	Asbāb	اسباب	To deceive	Dhoka dēnā	دھوکہ دینا
Ahead (*adv.*)	Āgē	آگے	Money	Rāqm	رقم

1. How much gram is given to the horse? 2. This table will be sent to your shop. 3. The matting of the room was changed last month. 4. The enemy was seen on the hill. 5. All the waste paper is thrown in the river. 6. If you make a noise again, you will be sent to the guard room. 7. One hundred men were sent there to clear the road. 8. When and where was the goat tied. 9. Are any tigers seen here? 10. The servants had been sent ahead to prepare dinner. 11. The effects of the soldier will be sold, and the money will be sent to his wife. 12. The old mares will be shot tomorrow.

The direct and Indirect Narrations

In English, there are two ways of repeating what somebody else had said; e.g.,

(1) The Direct Narration, when we use the speaker's actual words.

(2) The Indirect Narration, in which we repeat, what he said, in our own words.

In Urdu the Indirect Narration is uncommon and is confined to commands. It is much simple always to use the speaker's actual words, preceded by "keh" کہ *Inverted commas are not used in Urdu.*

The following examples will make this clear:—

Indirect: — John told me that he would go to Chittagong.

جان نے مجھ سے کہا کہ میں چٹگاؤں کو جاؤں گا

Direct : — John said to me, "I (John) will go to Chittagong.

John nē mujh sē kahā keh maiṅ (John) Chaṭgāoṅ ko jāūṅgā.

Indirect: — He asked me if my servant was in the room.

اس نے مجھ سے پوچھا کہ تمہارا نوکر کمرے میں ہے ؟

Direct: — He asked me, "Is your servant in the room?"

Us nē mujh sē pūchhā keh kia tumhārā naukar kamrē mēṅ hai?

Indirect: — The Colonel ordered him to open his box.

کرنل صاحب نے حکم دیا کہ اپنا صندوق کھولو

Direct : — The Colonel ordered him, "Open your box."

Karnēl sāheb nē usko hukm dīā keh apnā sandūq kholo.

Indirect : — He asked me if I was a teacher.

Direct : — He asked me, "Are you a teacher"

Us nē mujh sē pūchhā keh kīā āp Ustād haiṅ?

اس نے مجھ سے پوچھا کہ کیا آپ استاد ہیں ؟

EXERCISE 34(A)

Saudagar	Merchant	سوداگر	Batānā	To let know	بتانا
Zewar	Ornaments	زیور	Zarur	Without fail	ضرور

1. Us nē mujh sē pūchhā keh tum kahāṅ rahtē ho 2. Majīd sāheb nē mujh sē pūchhā keh tum is ādmī ko jāntē ho? 3. Bālṭiwālā sāheb nē darzī sē kahā keh maiṅ das bajē daftar ko aūṅgā. 4. Syed sāheb nē sipāhi sē pūchhā keh tum kab sē is ghar mēṅ rahtē ho? 5. Saudāgar nē mujh sē puchha keh tum nē yeh ghoṛā kab kharīdā hai? 6. Tum sē pūchhā jāegā keh yeh ghar kis

kē hukm sē banāyā gayā hai? 7. Mērē pās zarūr āo. 8. Ďākūoň nē ghar kē andar jā kar aurat sē pūchhā keh tumhārā zēwar kahāň hai, aur yeh bhī kahā keh agar tum nahīň batāogī to ham tumhārī bach-chī ko mār ďālēňgē.

EXERCISE 34(B)

Marriage	Shādī	شادی	To marry	Shādī karnā	شادی کرنا

1. He told me that he had fallen from the horse. 2. I asked him why he had come to me. 3. I told the man that I would give him ten rupees a month 4. The tailor says that you did not go to him. 5. He told me that he had come to my bungalow to see his brother. 6. The coolies asked me how much I had given to their head? 7. He told me that his servant would take me to the post office next morning. 8. The tailor told the butcher that he would take his money from him then and there. 9. Tell me what you read, and I will tell you what sort of man you are. 10. He told me that he was going to get married the following day. 11. She said to me that she did not know I was a farmer (Kisan)

Indirect Command

When an order is given indirectly (i.e., through a servant or some other person), the word "keh" (—that) is used after *kaho* or *bolo* (tell) or hukm do (order) etc. to introduce the actual command, and instead of the Imperative, we have the Aorist Tense (see page 95) of the Verb, agreeing in Number with the person or persons to whom the order is to be conveyed.

EXAMPLES

1. Tell the barber to wait.
   Tell the barber that (he) may wait.
   Haj-jām sē kaho keh thairē. حجّام سے کہو کہ ٹھہرے

2. Tell the boys to come here.
   Tell the boys that (they) may come here.
   Lařkoň sē kaho keh woh yahāň āēň. لڑکوں سے کہو کہ وہ یہاں آئیں

3. Order the syce to get the carriage ready.
Saīs ko hukm do keh gāṙī taīyār karē. سائیس کو حکم دو کہ گاڑی تیار کرے

4. Tell the men to cut this grass.
Ādmīoṅ sē kaho keh yeh ghāṅs kāṭēṅ آدمیوں سے کہو کہ یہ گھانس کاٹیں

EXERCISE 35(A)

Dawā *f.*	Medicine	دوا	Balke	But	بلکہ

1. Us sē kaho keh mujh ko rāstē mēṅ nahīṅ rokē. 2. Laṙkē sē kaho keh chiṭ-ṭhī apnē Sāheb kē pas lējāē 3. Chaukīdār sē kaho keh rāt ko nahīṅ soē. 4. Dhobī sē kaho keh hamārē kapṙē jaldī wāpas lāē. 5. Darzī sē kaho keh hamārī qamīsēṅ jaldī taīyār karē. 6. Chaukīdār sē kaho, keh agar yeh ādmī rāt ko hamārē baṅglē mēṅ aē, to is ko nahīṅ rokē. 7. Taxī wālē sē kaho, keh abhī taxī lējāē, aur das bajē wāpas lāē. 8. Mērē naukaroṅ ko samjhāo keh mujh sē Angrēzī kabhī nahīṅ bolēṅ balke hamēsha Urdu mēṅ bāt karēṅ. 9. Agar khidmatgār bīmār hai, to us sē kaho keh ḍākṭar sāheb kē pās jā kar dawā lāē. 10. Agar tum mērē naukar ko rāstē mēṅ dēkho, to us sē kaho keh jaldī mērē pās āē. 11. Sab naukaroṅ kī bīwīoṅ sē kaho keh rāt ko na to gāēṅ, aur na apnē bach-choṅ ko mārēṅ. 12. Laṙkoṅ sē kaho keh kūēṅ mēṅ pat-thar nahīṅ phēṅkēṅ. 13. Sāīs sē kaho keh is chiṭ-ṭhī kā jawāb mērē pās klab ko lāē. 14. Us sē kaho keh apnē sāheb ko hamārā salām dē. 15. Mālī sē kaho keh bahut bātēn na banāē aur jaisā hukm dīā gayā hai waisā karē.

EXERCISE 35(B)

Signature	Dast-khat	دستخط	To sign	Dast-khat karnā	دستخط کرنا
Account	Hisāb	حساب	Hair	Bāl	بال
Carefully	Hūshyārī sē	ہوشیاری سے	Cleverly	Hūshyārī sē	ہوشیاری سے

1. Tell him to open the box. 2. Tell the boy not to play on the verandah.

3. Tell the chaukidar to wake me up at 5 O'clock. 4. Tell the sweeper to bring the dog's food. 5. Tell them to come here tomorrow. 6. Tell the servant not to make a noise. 7. Tell the tailor to bring my clothes. 8. Tell the barber to cut my hair after dinner. 9. Tell the washerman to wash this shirt very carefully. 10. Call the servant and tell him to go and tell the barber not to come to me to day. 11. Tell this man not to show me his face again. 13. Tell the babu to bring the papers for signature. 14. Tell the chaprasi to call his saheb to the phone. 15. Tell him to go away now, and come back some other time. 16. Ask the saheb to sign the receipt, and send it back to me by post.

Participle Adjectives

The Present and Past Participles are commonly used as Adjectives to show the state or *condition* of the Noun before which they are used; as,

Present Participles	*Past Participles*
The *moving* train.	The *dead* horse.
The *dying* boy.	The *broken* table.

In the above examples "moving" and "dying" are Participles used as Adjectives, to show the state or condition of the "train" and the "boy" respectively.

In such cases "hūā" the Past Participle of the Verb "hona"-(to be), is added to the Present or Past Participles, as the case may be, to form the *Participle Adjectives*; as,

Present Participles			*Past Participles*		
Moving	Chaltā huā	چلتا ہوا	Dead	Mara huā	مرا ہوا
Dying	Mārta huā	مرتا ہوا	Broken	Ṭūṭā huā	ٹوٹا ہوا

EXAMPLES

1.	The moving train	Chaltī hūī gāṛī	چلتی ہوئی گاڑی
2.	From the sleeping man	Sotē hūē ādmī sē	سوتے ہوئے آدمی سے
3.	The dying boys	Martē hūē laṛkē	مرتے ہوئے لڑکے
4.	The dead horse	Marā hūā ghoṛā	مرا ہوا گھوڑا
5.	In the broken cup	Tūṭē hūē pīālē mēn̆	ٹوٹے ہوئے پیالے میں
6.	The burnt girl	Jalī hūī laṛkī	جلی ہوئی لڑکی

7. The dying boy gave me the address of his dead father written on a torn paper.
Martē hūē laṛkē nē mujh ko apnē marē hūē bāp kā patā ēk phaṭē hūē kāghaz par likhā hūā dīā.
مرتے ہوئے لڑکے نے مجھ کو اپنے مرے ہوئے باپ کا پتہ ایک پھٹے ہوئے کاغذ پر لکھا ہوا دیا

EXERCISE 36(A)

Dastūr	Custom	دستور	Bahādurī	Bravery	بہادری
Sabūt	Proof	ثبوت	Bāt	Matter, words	بات
Patta	Leaf	پتہ	Gawāhī	Evidence	گواہی
Kabūtar	Pigeon	کبوتر	Goli	Bullet	گولی
Kanjūs	Miser	کنجوس	Bhāgnā	To desert	بھاگنا
Pakaṛnā	To catch	پکڑنا	Dabnā	To be buried	دبنا
Dabānā	To bury	دبانا	Sūkhnā	To be dried	سوکھنا
Jama *k.*	To collect	جمع کرنا	Saṛnā	To be tainted	سڑنا
Barābar	Alike, equal	برابر	Khālī *Adj.*	Empty	خالی

1. Bahtā hūā pānī ach-chhā hotā hai. 2. Martē hūē dushman ko mārnā bahādurī nahīn̆ hai. 3. Tum nē jalī hūī roṭī khāī. 4. Sunī hūī bāt gawāhī kē liē kāfī sabūt nahīn̆ hai. 5. Bhāgā hūa sīpāhī apnē gāon̆ mēn̆ chhupā hūā pakṛā gayā. 6. Soyā hūā aur marā hūā ādmī barābar hotā hai. 7. Pānī pītē

hūē jānwar par golī chalānē kā dastūr nahīṅ hai. 8. Taīyār kīē hūē kapṛē tūṭē hūē sandūq mēṅ mat rakho. 9. Unhoṅ nē marī hūī ghoṛī ko jaṅgal mēṅ dabāyā. 10. Us nē uṛtē hūē kabūtaroṅ ko mār ḍālā. 11. Choroṅ nē sotē hūē ādmī ko rassī sē bāndhā 12. Sab sūkhī hūī roṭīāṅ uskī dukān ko wāpas bhējo. 13. Agar woh aurat dabā hūā khazāna na batātī to dākū uskē bachchē ko jaltī hūī āg mēṅ phēṅktē. 14. Darakhtoṅ kē girē hūē pat-tē ēk jaga jama kar kē jalāo. 15. Yeh botal bharī hūī hai, yā Khālī hai? 16. Ḍūbī hūī kishtī mēṅ do tūṭī hūī gāṛīāṅ bhī thīṅ. 17. Tum yeh saṛā hūā gosht kīā karogē? 18. Kanjūs ādmī kē bēṭē nē apnē bāp kā jama kīā hūā sab rupīa thoṛē din mēṅ barbād kīā. 19. Chale hūē kārtūs, bharē hūē kārtūsoṅ sē alag rakho.

EXERCISE 36(B)

Ship	Jahāz	جہاز	Crew	Jahāz kā Amla	جہاز کا عملہ
Beggar	Faqīr	فقیر	Law	Qānūn	قانون
Cowardly *adj.*	Ḍarpok	ڈرپوک	Cavalry	Risāla	رسالہ
Leg *f.*	Tāṅg	ٹانگ	Kettle *f.*	Kētlī	کیتلی
To be broken	Tūṭnā	ٹوٹنا	To jump	Kūdnā	کودنا
To fill	Bharnā	بھرنا	To hurl	De mārnā	دے مارنا
To be boiling	Khaulnā	کھولنا	Unwritten	Unlikhā	ان لکھا
To be drowned	Dūbnā	ڈوبنا	To sink	Dūbnā	ڈوبنا

1. I went into the burning room to save the crying child. 2. He took off his burnt clothes. 3. The thief jumped from the moving train. 4. Two boats were sent to save the crew of the sinking ship. 5. Our cavalry attacked the retreating enemy. 6. I have seen it written somewhere. 7. The sentry stopped the running horse. 8. My cowardly servant would not go near the dead tiger. 9. They brought the drowned man to me. 10. The wounded soldier showed

me his broken leg. 1. He hurled the glass full of beer at the beggar's head. 12. Bring some boiling water in the kettle. 13. This is an unwritten law.

REVISIONAL EXERCISE 37(A)

(On Exercises from 30 to 36)

Words

Artillery	Top khāna	توپ خانہ	Hole, pit	Gaṙhā	گڑھا
Property	Māl; Milkīat	مال؍ملکیت	Word	Lafz	لفظ
Generally	Aksar	اکثر	Fast (sleep)	Bē khabar	بے خبر
Whole (all)	Sab	سب	Whole (unbroken)	Sābut	ثابت
To dig	Khodnā	کھودنا	Gun (cannon)	Top	توپ
Line	Lāin *f.*	لائن	To stand	Khaṙā honā	کھڑا ہونا
To load	Bharnā	بھرنا	To drive back	Pīchhē haṭānā	پیچھے ہٹانا
To post	Dāk mēn̐ dālnā	ڈاک میں ڈالنا	To make haste	Jaldī karnā	جلدی کرنا
To be torn			To count	Ginnā	گننا
To burst	Phaṭnā	پھٹنا			

REVISIONAL EXERCISE 37(A)

(On Exercises from 30 to 36)

1. Put an anna stamp on this letter and post it. 2. Bring the receipt with you tomorrow morning at eight. 3. Tell the boy to make haste. 4. Ask him if he has come to put the fan right. 5. He was asked to call at another time. 6. You forget to do everything, do you ever forget to have your food (bread)? 7. To steal is not a crime but to be caught is one. 8. The enemy was driven back with the help of the artillery. 9. The thieves dug a hole in the ground to bury the stolen property. 10. Giving is better than receiving. 11. The child

dropped the loaded gun, which went off at once. 12. Two guns were hidden behind the trees. 13. I taught him both reading and writing. 14. He was taught both reading and writing. 15. There is no pleasure in going so fast. 16. Did I make a mistake in counting the words? 17. You make ten mistakes in writing five lines. 18. Ask him if he has brought the bill. 19. Tell them to be quiet. 20. Although he was fast asleep, his eyes were open. 21. Home-made sweets are generally the most delicious. 22. As the pocket was torn, the rupee fell out somewhere. 23. Looking for the lost rupee along the road I reached my bungalow, where I saw it lying under a burnt paper. 24. You said, you did not know the dead man, how do you know that he is a runaway soldier? 25. When the shell burst the soldiers standing up were wounded, those lying down escaped. 26. Bring some hot water to wash my hands. 27. Is this cup broken or whole? 28. He abused my dead mother.

REVISIONAL EXERCISE 37(B)

۱۔ لڑکے نے آپ اپنی گھڑی توڑی ہے۔ ۲۔ غریب عورتیں اپنے گھر کا کام آپ کرتی ہیں۔ ۳۔ میرا سائیس آپ کے گھوڑے کے واسطے گھانس نہیں لائے گا۔ ۴۔ مولوی صاحب نے خود تم کو باغ میں دیکھا تھا۔ ۵۔ تم تیرنا جانتے ہو۔ ۶۔ بہادر آدمی مرنے اور مارنے سے نہیں ڈرتے ہیں۔ ۷۔ ہر وقت ہنسنا اور روالٹ نکالنا بہت خراب عادتیں ہیں۔ ۸۔ بات کرنا آسان ہے لیکن کام کرنا بڑا مشکل ہے۔ ۹۔ آپ کا نوکر آپ کو بلانے آیا ہے۔ ۱۰۔ تم یہاں سیکھنے کو آئے ہو یا سکھانے کو۔ ۱۱۔ یہ دو روپے تمہارے مٹھائی کھانے کے ہیں۔ ۱۲۔ خدا نے دن کام کرنے کو اور رات آرام کرنے کو بنائی ہے۔ ۱۳۔ تمہاری عرضی جج صاحب کے سامنے رکھی جائے گی۔ ۱۴۔ ڈاکوؤں نے گھر کے اندر جا کر عورت سے پوچھا کہ تمہارا زیور کہاں ہے اور یہ بھی کہا کہ اگر تم نہیں بتاؤ گی تو ہم تمہاری بچی کو مار ڈالیں گے۔ ۱۵۔ مالی سے کہو کہ بہت باتیں نہ بنائے اور جیسا حکم دیا گیا ہے ویسا کرے۔

PART IV

This Part comprises those Verbs which follow particular rules when joined to, or used with, other Verbs in the same sentence.

The Verbs "Sakn ā" سکنا and "Chukn ā" چُکنا

Saknā— To be able	Are joined to the "*root*" of the
Chuknā— To finish	Verb, whose action they govern.

EXAMPLES

1. To be able to write	Likh saknā	لکھ سکنا
2. To be able to see	Dēkh saknā	دیکھ سکنا
3. To have done writing	Likh chuknā	لکھ چکنا
4. To finish playing	Khēl chuknā	کھیل چکنا

Note :— The Verbs, "Sakn ā" and "Chukn ā" are conjugated to show the required Tense, while the roots, to which they are added, undergo no change.

EXAMPLES

1. I am able to go there (or) I can go there — Maiň wahāň jā saktā hūň.
2. She was not able to speak Arabic or She could not speak Arabic — Woh Arbī nahīň bol saktī thī.
3. We shall not be able to come to you tomorrow.
   Ham kal tumhārē pās nahīň a sakēňgē
4. Have you finished writing the mail?
   Tum d̄āk (or khat) likh chukē ho?
5. The girls will finish playing presently.
   Laŕkiāň thoŕī dēr mēň khēl chukēňgī.

EXERCISE 38(A)

Marzī f.	Consent, willingness	مرضی
Andhērā	Dark	اندھیرا
Hargiz nahīṅ	Never or under no circumstances	ہرگز نہیں

1. Maiṅ āj tumhārē pās nahīṅ ā saktā hūṅ 2. Woh aisā mahṅgā ghoṛā nahīṅ k͟harīd saktā hai 3. Laṛkī tumhārī marzī kē bag͟hair tum ko chiṭ-ṭhī nahīṅ bhēj saktī hai. 4. Ham yeh purānī chīzēṅ Sāheb kē hukm kē bag͟hair nahīṅ bēch saktē haiṅ. 5. Tum abhī do mahīnē tak chhuṭ-ṭī pār hargiz nahīṅ jā sakogē. 6. Tum mat ḍaro, who tum ko nahīṅ mār saktē haiṅ. 7. Maiṅ yeh kitāb paṛh chukā hūṅ, ab tum isko (paṛhnē kē wāstē) lējā saktē ho. 8. Woh apnā ghoṛā bēch chukā hai, ab woh usko wāpas nahīṅ lē saktā hai. 9. K͟hālid sāheb sab kāg͟hazoṅ par dastk͟hat kar chukē haiṅ, ab shāyad woh apne baṅgle ko jāēṅgē. 10. Agar auratēṅ ghāṅs kāt chukī haiṅ, to un sē kaho keh woh ab jā saktī haiṅ.

EXERCISE 38(B)

Experience	Tajriba	تجربہ	Rain	Bārish	بارش

1. My servant can go with you. 2. I could not come here yesterday on account of the rain. 3. I cannot send my servant to you everyday. 4. You cannot forget his name. 5. She cannot write Urdu. 6. We cannot read this letter. 7. Will you be able to play next week? 8. They will not be able to catch the thief in the dark. 9. I have finished writing my letters, now I can go with you. 10. Go and see if the men have finished eating 11. Take this letter to the treasury, if you have finished cleaning the room. 12. The girl has finished making the tea. 13. Only experience can teach you this. 14. No one can do two things at the same time.

CHĀHNĀ (چاہنا)

The Verb "CHĀHNĀ" — To wish, to want, etc.

In English the Verb "to wish" is used within an Infinitive and in the same way "*Chāhnā*" takes the infinitive *before it* in Urdu; as,

To wish to eat	Khānā chāhnā	کھانا چاہنا
To wish to go	Jānā chāhnā	جانا ۔ چاہنا
To wish to see	Dēkhnā chāhnā	دیکھنا ۔ چاہنا

1. I wish to play this evening.
   Maiṅ āj shām ko khēlnā chāhtā hūṅ.
   میں آج شام کو کھیلنا چاہتا ہوں
2. She wishes to go to the dance.
   Woh nāch mēṅ jānā chāhtī hai.
   وہ ناچ میں جانا چاہتی ہے
3. They were not desirous of waiting.
   Woh ṭhairnā nahīṅ chāhtē thē.
   وہ ٹھہرنا نہیں چاہتے تھے ۔
4. He will not want to sleep here.
   Woh yahāṅ sonā nahīṅ chāhēgā.
   وہ یہاں سونا نہیں چاہے گا
5. Do you want to buy this tractor?
   Tum yeh tractor kharīdnā chāhtē ho?
   تم یہ ٹریکٹر خریدنا چاہتے ہو ؟

EXERCISE 39(A)

Fauj *f.*	Army	فوج	Aksar *Adj.*	Most	اکثر
Hazār	Thousand	ہزار	Aksar *Adv.*	Often	اکثر

1. Maiṅ apnī bīwī kē pās tār bhējnā chāhtā hūṅ. 2. Woh aglē haftē

shikār ko jānā chāhtā hai. 3. Uskī bēṭī hoṭal mēn̈ rahnā nahīn̈ chāhtī hai. 4. Ham do hazār rupai qarz lēnā chāhtē hain̈. 5. Woh apnē nām Pākistānī palṭan kē wāstē dēnā chāhtē hain̈. 6. Woh lar̈kā apnā khat kisī ko dikhānā nahīn̈ chāhtā hai. 7. Sab naukar tamāsha dēkhnē ko jānā chāhēn̈gē. 8. Apnē shahr jānā kaun chāhtā hai? 9. Woh aisē badmāsh hain̈ kēh tumhārē kapr̈ē bhī utārnē chāhēn̈gē 10. Dushman kā jāsūs apnī fauj ko hamārā risālē kē ānē kī khabar dēnā chāhtā hai. 11. Āj kal har ēk ādmī motar chalānā sīkhnā chāhtā hai. 12. Hamārē ādmī bahut sawērē rawāna honā chāhtē thē. 13. Tum is bāt ko chhupānā kion̈ chāhtē ho? 14. Woh apnī rasīdēn̈ wāpas lēnā chāhēgā. 15. Aksar naukar apnē sāheb kē sāth apnē shahr sē bāhar jānā nahīn̈ chāhtē hain̈. 16. Agar tum chhuṭ-ṭī par jānā chāhtē ho, to kām karnē kē wāstē dūsrā ādmī lāo.

EXERCISE 39(B)

Country	Mulk	ملک	Contract	Thēka	ٹھیکہ
Else; more	Aur	اور	Peace	Sulah	صلح
Alive	Zinda	زندہ	To capture	Pakar̈nā	پکڑنا
To pay	Adā karnā	ادا کرنا	Front (war)	Lar̈āī, maidān-e-jan̈g	لڑائی/میدان جنگ

1. I wish to go to the front to fight for my country. 2. I do not want to see your face again. 3. The thief wished to escape. 4. The woman wishes to go by the mail train. 5. The enemy wishes to make peace. 6. They will not want to come here again. 7. Do you want to take all these contracts? 8. Do you wsih to deceive me? 9. Why does he want to see me? 10. Why do you want to know that? 11. We wished to capture the spy alive. 12. I would like to have a talk with you. 13. My father wishes to take my servants with him to Kashmir. 14. I wish to pay off my debts this month. 15. I want to ask you once more. 16. What else do they want?

CHĀHĪÉ (چاہیئے)

"Chāhie" is the respectful Imperative of "Chahna" and is used in the sense of *should* and *ought* and also *must* in a mild sense.

"Chā hīē" takes its subject in the dative case, (e.g. *ko* is used after the subject) and the Principal Verb in the Infinitive; as

EXAMPLES

1. I should go (or) It is upon me to go.
   (To me, to go, should) — Mujh ko jānā chāhīē.

   مجھ کو جانا چاہیے

2. The men should not have come here.
   Ādmīoň ko yahāň nahīň ānā chāhīē thā.

   آدمیوں کو یہاں نہیں آنا چاہیے تھا

Observation:— If the accompanying. Verb is transitive and has an object, the idiom differs at Lucknow and Delhi. (Vide note on next page).

At Lucknow the "Infinitive coupled with the direct object" is treated as a compound Verb, and hence the infinitive is never inflected. The Plural Form *chahien* is never used at Lucknow, and is rather detested.

Delhi people make the Infinitive agree with the object in Gender and Number, and use the Plural Form *chahien* to agree with the object in Number.

EXAMPLES

1. The man should bring three horses.
   Ādmī ko tīň ghoṙē lānā chāhīē. (Lucknow)
   Ādmī ko tīň ghoṙē lānē chāhīēň (Delhi).

2. You should sell this mare.
   Tum ko yeh ghoṙī bēchnā chāhīē. (Lucknow)
   Tum ko yeh ghoṙī bēchnī chāhīē. (Delhi)

3. I should learn several languages
   Mujh ko kaī zabānēň sīkhnā chāhīē. (Lucknow)
   Mujh ko kaī zabānēň sīkhnī chāhīēň. (Delhi)

Note :— In the Past Tense "chā hīē" is followed by the past auxiliaries e.g. "th ā, thē or thī" etc.; as,

4. He ought to have bought two locks.
Unko do tālē kharīdnā chāhīē thē. (Lucknow)
Unko do tālē kharīdnē chāhīēṅ thē. (Delhi)

They ought to have seen the carriage
Unko gāṛī dēkhnā chāhīē thī. (Lucknow)
Unko gāṛī dēkhnī chāhīē thī. (Delhi).

* There is another construction which is everywhere the same. In it chāhīē followed by "keh" starts the sentence, and the principal Verb is put in the Aorist, which agrees in number with the subject (and not with the object); as,

1. I should go.
It is necessary that I should go (may go).
Chāhīē keh maiṅ jāūṅ.

2. The boys should come here.
Chāhīē keh laṛkē yahāṅ āēṅ.

Note :— In the Past Tense "Chāhīē thā" is followed by the Past Conditional, as,

1. I should have gone there
Chāhīē thā keh maiṅ wahāṅ jātā.

2. You should have shown the mare to me.
Chāhīē thā keh tum ghoṛī mujh ko dikhātē.

Note :— *The different constructions about the use of "Chāhīē" are given above. The student may choose whichever idiom he thinks convenient to adopt. If he knows the other two he will be quite at case when he comes across them in writing or speech.

EXERCISE 40(A)

1. Mujh ko us kē sāth rahnā nahīṅ chāhīē. 2. Us ko apnē dost kē sāth

aisā salūk karnā nahīṅ chāhīē. 3. Tum ko apnī chīzēṅ sandūq mēṅ rakh kar tālā lagānā chāhīē. 4. Ham ko naukar kē sāth mazāq nahīṅ karnā chāhīē. 5. Shahr kē logoṅ ko āpas mēṅ hargiz nahīṅ laṙnā chāhīē. 6. Tum ko kisī dūsrē ādmī kā khat hargiz nahīṅ paṙhnā chāhīē. 7. Tum ko apnē paṙausīoṅ ko nāhaq nuqsān pahuṅhcānā nahīṅ chāhīē. 8. Sab ādmīoṅ ko apnē kām par waqt sē pāṅch miniṭ pahlē pahuṅchnā chāhīē. 9. Tum ko apnā kām bahut hūshyārī sē karnā chāhīē. 10. Auratoṅ ko āj kal rāt ko nau bajē kē bād bāzār mēṅ nikalnā nahīṅ chāhīē. 11. Uskī bēṭīoṅ ko naukaroṅ kī bīwīoṅ sē laṙnā nahīṅ chāhīē. 12. Bāwarchī ko mailā pānī rāstē mēṅ nahīṅ phēṅknā chāhīē thā. 13. Sipāhī ko aisī chiṭ-ṭhī apnē afsar ko nahīṅ likhnī chāhīē. 14. Aqlmand ādmī ko āj kā kām kal par nahīṅ chhoṙnā chāhīē. 15. Chāhīē thā keh tum ṭūṭī hūī botal kē tukṙē farsh par nahīṅ rahnē dētē.

EXERCISE 40(B)

1. You should not come inside the office. 2. They should not make a noise. 3. What should we do then? 4. The chowkidar should not sleep at night. 5. What a fool, you must have patience. 6. The girls should not read such books. 7. You should not show your mistake to the people. 8. The man should not spread false rumours in the bazaar. 9. The papers should not be burnt near the grass. 10. All the recruits should clean their rifles everyday. 11. You should not steal Government property. 12. We ought not to have killed the peacocks. 13. They should not have cut these green trees.

"PAṘNĀ" (پڑنا) AND "HON Ā" (ہونا)

The Verb "Paṙnā" and "Hon ā" are added to the Infinitive to give sense of "Must", "to have to" etc. They also require their subject in the dative, and follow exactly the same rules as "ch āhīē" regarding the agreement of the Infnitive with the object.

"Paṙnā" پڑنا is used to show absolute compulsion or to have to do anything against one's convenience, per force, or when there is no alternative.

"Hon ā" ہونا is used to show when a thing is decided upon or arranged, supposed to be done or is advisable.

In short

Pařna shows that a thing *has* to be done.

Hona shows that a thing *is* to be done; as,

1. I was to go there yesterday.
   Mujh ko kal wahāň jānā thā.

2. I had to go there yesterday.
   Mujh ko kal wahāň jānā pařā.

3. The thief had to confess his crime.
   Chor ko apnā jurm mānnā pařā. (No alternative)

4. The woman will have to go.
   Aurat ko jānā hogā. (arranged)
   Aurat ko jānā pařēgā. (must)

5. I have to buy a good mare.
   Mujh ko ēk ach-chhī ghořī kharīdnā hai. (Lucknow)
   Mujh ko ēk ach-chhī ghořī kharīdnī hai. (Delhi)

6. I have to see the horses everyday.
   Mujh ko har roz ghořē dēkhnā hotē haiň. (arranged)
   Mujh ko har roz ghořē dēkhnā pařtē haiň. (must)
   Mujh ko har roz ghořē dēkhnē pařtē haiň (Delhi)

7. You will have to give him his pay.
   Tum ko uskī tankhwāh dēnā hogī (decision)
   Tum ko uskī tankhwāh dēnā pařēgī (must)
   Tum ko uskī tankhwāh dēnī pařēgī (Delhi)

EXERCISE 41(A)

1. Tum ko yeh khaiāb dānā wāpas lēnā paṙēgā, aur iskī qīmat wāpas dēnī paṙēgī. 2. Tum ko uskē sāth kām karnā paṙēgā. 3. Sāṅpoṅ kē sabab ham ko yeh baṅgla chhoṙnā paṙēgā. 4. Maiṅ yahāṅ ēk din kē wāstē āyā thā, lēkin shāyad mujh ko tīn din tak ṭhairnā paṙēgā. 5. Tum ko mērē sāth laṙāī par chalnā paṙēgā. 6. Mujh ko kuchh chīzēṅ kharīdnē bāzār jānā hai. 7. Tum ko palṭan kē sāth laṙāī par jānā hogā. 8. Apnē dost ko sazā sē bachānē kē wāstē mujh ko jhūt bolnā paṙēgā, lēkin maiṅ jhūt bolnā nahīṅ chāhtā hūṅ. 9. General sāheb ko daurē par jānā hai. 10. Agar tum ko jānā hai to jāo; maiṅ tum ko rok nahīṅ saktā hūṅ. 11. Tum ko kia khabar keh ham ko laṙāī par kiā kiā dēkhnā paṙtā hai.

EXERCISE 41(B)

1. Every child in India has got to go to school. 2. I have to go to see my friend. 3. He had to wait there for orders. 4. Thou *shalt* not steal. 5. They had to take off their clothes for the medical inspection. 6. The soldiers are to obey their officers' orders. 7. You will have to buy warm clothes yourself. 8. You will have to put all these things in the sun at least once a week. 9. I have to send these boxes to Delhi by passenger train. 10. Bearer, you should stay on the verandah, for if you are not there, I have to come out of the room to call you. 11. He has to spend two hundred rupees a month.

The Verb "MILNĀ" (ملنا)

The Verb "Milnā" ' ملنا, stands for several English Verbs such as, to get, to find, to receive, to obtain, to meet and to come across, etc. etc.

The construction is the reverse of that used in English, the subject being in the Dative and the object, with which the Verb agrees in gender and number, in the Nominative case.

EXAMPLES

1. I received a letter. مجھ کو ایک چٹھی ملی
(By me a letter was received)—Mujh ko ēk chiṭ-ṭhī milī.
2. The man got two horses — Ādmī ko do ghoṛē milē.
آدمی کو دو گھوڑے ملے
3. She will get a reward — Us ko inām milēgā. اس کو انعام ملے گا
4. Did you find all the things correct?
Kiā tum ko sab chīzēṅ ṭhīk milīṅ? کیا تم کو سب چیزیں ٹھیک ملیں
5. You cannot get more than two days' leave.
Tum ko do din sē ziāda kī chhuṭ-ṭī nahīṅ mil sakti.
تم کو دو دن سے زیادہ کی چھٹی نہیں مل سکتی

EXERCISE 42(A)

Dūdh	Milk	دودھ	Kinārā	Bank, shore	کنارا
Pās	Pass	پاس	Zīada	More (*Adj.*)	زیادہ
Wardī	Uniform	وردی	Jhāṛī	Bush	جھاڑی
Qismat	Luck	قسمت	Kam	Less	کم

1. Ham ko yahāṅ bahut ach-chhā dūdh nahīṅ miltā hai. 2. Pahlā inām sab sē bahādur ādmī ko milēgā. 3. Aglē mahīnē mēṅ sipāhīoṅ ko naī wardīāṅ milēṅgī 4. Tum ko mērī jēb mēṅ sē koī chhoṭī kitāb milī hai? 5. Mērē bēṭē ko yeh anḍē jhāṛī mēṅ milē thē. 6. Āj kal laṛāī kē sabab wilāyatī chīzēṅ nahīṅ mil saktī haiṅ. 7. Tum ko mērā pata kaisē milā? 8. Mērē naukar ko āj chār bajē kē bād khānā milā hai. 9. Sāheb ko zīn pul kē nīchē paṛī hūī milī. 10. Tumhārē bhāī ko daftar sē kiā miltā hai? 11. Ham ko rāstē mēṅ bahut ādmī auratēṅ aur bach-chē milē jo shahr ko chīzēṅ kharīdnē kē wāstē jā rahē thē. 12. Jo kuchh tumhārī qismat mēṅ likhā hūā hai tum ko us sē ziāda nahīṅ mil saktā. 13. Qile kē andar jānē kā pās nahīṅ miltā hai? 14. Hoṭal mēṅ bahut sāheb haiṅ, ham ko kamrē nahīṅ mil sakēṅgē. 15. Tum ko

arzī kā kuchh jawāb milā? 16. Yeh laṙkē mujh ko bāgh mēṅ ghāṅs par lēṭē hūē milē. 17. Dhobī kī bēṭīoṅ ko yeh laṙkī daryā kē kinārē kē pās roti hūī milī.

EXERCISE 42(B)

Medal	Tamgha	تمغہ	Cross-road	Chaurāhā	چوراہا
Bunch	Guch-chhā	گچھا	Hard work	Mehnat *f.*	محنت
No body	Koī nahīṅ	کوئی نہیں	Almirah	Almārī *f.*	الماری
Frontier	Sarhad	سرحد	Jew, Jewess	Yahūdī, yahūdan	یہودی/یہودن

1. The brave solider received a medal in the last war. 2. I found this bunch of keys lying near the Jew's house. 3. When did you receive my letter? 4. Did you find the mistake in your account? 5. The regiment got an order to go to the Frontier at once. 6. If you work properly, you will get a reward. 7. My servant could not find the teacher's house. 8. How much do you get in a month? 9. I shall not get such a good servant again. 10. The police found all the things hidden behind the almirah in the shop. 11. These men cannot get the contract now. 12. Nothing is obtained in the world without hard work. 13. You will find nobody here to day. 14. If you meet my servant on the way, please tell him I have found the watch, and that he should come to me at once.

LAGNĀ PĀNĀ لگنا، پانا AND DĒNĀ دینا

Lagnā	To begin	لگنا	Take the inflected form of the accompanying Infinitive.
Pānā	To be allowed:	پانا	
Dēnā	To allow; to let	دینا	

Note *:— The word "ijāzat" (permission) is understood with "dēnā" and "pānā".*

1.	To begin to eat	Khānē lagnā	کھانے لگنا
2.	To be allowed to go	Jānē pānā	جانے پانا
3.	To allow to sleep	Sonē dēnā	سونے دینا

4. He began to open the box.
Woh sandūq kholnē lagā.

5. I have begun to understand now.
Maiň ab samajhnē lagā hūň.

6. You will begin to speak Urdu in two months.
Tum do mahīnē mēň Urdu bolnē lagogē.

7. He will not be allowed to keep a rifle.
Woh rāifal rakhnē nahīň pāēgā.

8. We are not allowed to go there.
Ham wahāň jānē nahīň pātē haiň.

9. Let him bring the horse here.
Usko ghořā yahāň lānē do.

Note:— It must be remembered that "Dēnā", being a Transitive Verb, requires the use of "nē" with the subject in the past tense.

10. Mr. Mirza did not allow him to buy the horse.
Mirzā sāheb nē usko ghořā nahīň Kharīdnē dīā.

11. He did not let me read the letter
Us nē mujh ko chiţ-ţhī nahīň pařhnē dī.

EXERCISE 43(A)

Kawwā	Crow	کوّا	Thēkēdār	Contractor	ٹھیکیدار
Murghī	Hen	مرغی	Waghaira	Etcetera	وغیرہ
Ke siwāē	Except	کے سوائے	Māň bāp	Parents (māň - mother; bāp - father)	ماں باپ

1. Woh ab Urdu samajhnē lagā hai. 2. Jab woh lařkī apnē khāwind kē ghar jānē lagī to us kē māň bāp muskurānē lagē. 3. Jab mērī gāřī chalnē

lagēgī to kuttā bhauṅknē lagēgā. 4. Maiṅ apnē palaṅg par lēṭ kar ēk kitāb paṛhnē lagā. 5. Ab tum itnā jhūṭ kioṅ bolnē lagē ho? 6. Yeh bach-cha shāyad do tīn mahīnē mēṅ chalnē lagēgā. 7. Yeh sust ādmī mujh ko dēkh kar kām karnē lagtē haiṅ. 8. Jab kawwē koī sāṅp dēkhtē haiṅ to bahut chil-lānē aur shor karnē lagtē haiṅ. 9. Maiṅ tum ko un ādmīoṅ kē pās nahīṅ jānē dūṅgā, agar tum jāogē to unko ghar mēṅ nahīṅ pāogē. 10. Tum mujh ko sonē kīoṅ nahīṅ dētē ho? 11. Mērē hukm kē baghair kisī ādmī ko yahāṅ mat rahnē do. 12. Naukar baṅglē mēṅ bakrī aur murghi waghaira nahīṅ rakhnē pāēṅgē. 13. Chapṛāsī inām kē baghair thēkēdār ko sāheb kē sāmnē nahīṅ jānē degā. 14. Woh apnē dostoṅ ko chiṭ-ṭhīāṅ bhējnē nahīṅ pāēgā. 15. Afsaroṅ kē siwāē koī ādmī is jaṅgal mēṅ shikār khēlnē nahīṅ pātā hai 16. Do haftē tak kisī ādmī ko is kūēṅ sē pānī mat lēnē do.

EXERCISE 43(B)

Villager	Gāoṅ wālā	گاؤں والا	Sweeper	Mehtar; bhaṅgī	مہتر، بھنگی
Peacock	Mor; mornī *f.*	مور، مورنی	Properly	Ṭhīk ṭhīk (*adv.*)	ٹھیک ٹھیک
To abuse	Gālī dēnā	گالی دینا	To touch	Chhūnā	چھونا
To take in	Bēwaqūf banānā	بیوقوف بنانا			
To let go, *to allow to go*	Jānē dēnā	جانے دینا	To let go (*release*)	Chhoṛnā	چھوڑنا

1. When I go to him for pay, he begins to abuse me. 2. She begins to read very early. 3. Having seen him, all the women began to laugh. 4. The servants have begun to take me in. 5. When will you begin to work properly? 6. He is not allowed to walk about. 7. We are not allowed to leave the office before 2 o'clock. 8. Let the officer go to bazaar to buy some things. 9. Let the dog go. 10. He was allowed to sleep in the office. 11. They will be allowed to see their friends. 12.Do not let the sweeper touch my things. 13. The dog will not let any man come near the room. 14. The villagers did not allow us to shoot peacocks. 15. The doctor allowed him to eat meat. 16. I cannot allow you to open his letter.

The Habitual Tense

The Habitual Tense shows that the action is done regularly, habitually as a rule. as, He used to go.

In Urdu, the Habitual Tense is formed by adding the verb "karnā" (to do), to the *Past Participle* of the Verb. The Past Participle always remains unchanged, while the Verb "karna" is conjugated to show the required tense; as,

To be in the habit of sleeping	Soyā karnā	سویا کرنا
To be accustomed to walk	Chalā karnā	چلا کرنا
To be in the habit of going	Jāyā* karnā (*not* gayā karnā)	جایا کرنا

* The Verb jana takes its regular Past Participle "jāyā" (and not gayā) before "karnā"

EXAMPLES

1. I am in the habit of rising very early.
   Maiṅ bahut sawērē uṭhā kartā hūṅ.

2. I used to buy everything from his shop.
   Maiṅ har chīz uskī dūkān sē kharīdā kartā thā.

3. Make it a habit to give the horse some salt every day.
   Ghoṛē ko har roz namak diā karo.

4. A mare used to graze in the jungle.
   Ek ghoṛī jaṅgal mēṅ charā kartī thī.

5. What time will you come to me every day?
   Tum har roz kis waqt mērē pās āyā karogē?

Note :— Sometimes in Urdu, as in English, the Present Indefinite and Past Imperfect Tenses are used as habitual tenses; as

6. Ahmad talks too much, but works very little.
   Ahmad bāt bahut zīāda kartā hai, lēkin kām bahut thoṙā kartā hai.

7. Waheed and Rafi were always laughing at him.
   Waheed aur Rafi us par hamēsha haṅstē thē.

EXERCISE 44(A)

Nāshta	Breakfast	ناشتہ	Darja	Class	درجہ
Guldasta	Bouquet	گلدستہ	Gadhā	Ass	گدھا
Rīwālwar	Revolver	ریوالور	Safar karnā	To travel	سفر کرنا
Dhonā	To wash	دھونا	Dakhl dēnā	To meddle	دخل دینا
Sinā	To sew	سینا			

1. Hindū gosht nahīṅ khāyā kartē haiṅ. 2. Qilē kā darzī mērē kapṙē sīā kartā hai. 3. Qasāī har roz shām ko aglē din kē wāstē hukm lēnē āyā kartā hai. 4. Sipāhī har sāl chhuṭ-ṭī pār apnē gharoṅ ko jāyā kartē haiṅ. 5. Tum nāshta kis waqt kartē ho? 6. Uskī bīwī har roz shām ko klab jā kar ṭēnis khēlā kartī hai. 7. Daftar kē darwāzē kaun kholtā hai? 8. Jab maiṅ khēl kar wāpas ātā hūṅ, to ghusl kīā kartā hūṅ. 9. Tum apnā qasūr hamēsha dūsrē naukaroṅ par rakhtē ho. 10. Paṭhān bahut bahādurī sē laṙā kartē haiṅ. 11. Maiṅ apnē takyē kē nīchē rīwālwar rakh kar soyā kartā hūṅ. 12. Jab do pahr hotī hai to dhobī kī bīwī uskē līē khānā lāyā kartī hai. 13. Tumhārē kapṙē kaunsā dhobī dhoyā kartā hai. 14. Mālī har roz mērē wāstē do guldastē lāyā kartā thā. 15. Kīā kābul mēṅ gadhē nahīṅ hūā kartē haiṅ? 16. Woh bēwaqūf ādmī hamēsha dūsroṅ kī bāt mēṅ dakhl dīā kartā hai. 17. Tum sharāb pīā kartē ho.

EXERCISE 44(B)

Compound	Ehāta	احاطہ	Fair	Mēla	میلہ
To take an exercise		Warzish karnā	ورزش کرنا		

1. This man used to bring my mail from the post office. 2. My servant's children used to make a great noise in the compound. 3. Do not accustom yourself to telling lies. 4. Ask them why they always laugh at me? 5. A tiger used to carry away men and women who were returning after dark from the city. 6. The wives and the daughters of the servants used to sing at night. 7. I am in the habit of taking a bath twice daily. 8. In future all the receipts will be sent to the treasury. 9. A large fair used to take place there every year. 10. Why are you always joking with my old servant? 11. Two men used to live in the same house, and used to drink wine and fight a good deal with each other. 12. The wicked man, who used to steal horses, has been caught. 13. I shall make it a habit to take some exercise every evening.

The Continual Tense

The Continual Tense is expressed in the following two ways:—

(i) The Verb "rahnā" (to remain) is joined to the *Present Participle* of any other Verb. The Present Participle changes its final "a" into "e" or "i" according to the Number and Gender of the subject; as,

To keep on writing	Likhtē rahnā.
He kept on writing	Woh likhtā rahā.
She keeps on writing	Woh likhtī rahtī hai.
We shall keep on writing	Ham likhtē rahēṅgē.
The girls shall keep on writing	Laṛkīāṅ likhtī rahēṅgī.

(2) The Verb "jānā" (to go on) is added to the Inflected Past Participle of the Verb. The Past Participle is always in the inflected form and never changes; as,

To keep on writing	Likhē jānā.
He kept on writing	Woh likhē gāyā.

She keeps on writing	Woh likhē jātī hai.
We shall keep on writing	Ham likhē jāēṅgē.
You keep on writing (*Present*)	Tum likhē jātē ho.
You keep on writing (*Command*)	Tum likhē jāo.

Note:— The two constructions have not, strictly speaking, precisely the same meaning. "Rahnā" expresses merely continuity of action; "jānā", on the other hand, is used when the action is continued inspite of some possible cause of interruption. Thus "she goes on writing all day long" would be "rahnā"; but "when I entered the room he kept on with his work", would be "jānā"

EXERCISE 45(A)

Vakīl	Pleader	وکیل	Sūrā<u>kh</u>; chhēd	Hole	سوراخ/چھید
Koshish	Effort	کوشش	Mana karnā	To forbid	منع کرنا
Paṙausī	Neighbour	پڑوسی	Pāgal	Mad	پاگل
Kāmyāb	Successful	کامیاب	Din bhar	All day	دن بھر
Chupkā	Quietly	چپکا	Barābar	Continually	برابر
Paṙaus	Neighbourhood	پڑوس	Musībat	Mishap, trouble	مصیبت

1. Paṭhān sarhad par hamēsha taīyār rahtē hain. 2. Tumhārā bēṭā mērē bētē kē sāth bahut dēr tak khēltā rahā. 3. Hamārā vakīl jaj sāheb kē sāmnē do ghanṭē tak barābar boltā rahā. 4. Chor ēk ghanṭē tak dīwār mēṅ sūrā<u>kh</u> kartē rahē. 5. Naukaroṅ kī bīwīāṅ kal subah sē shām tak laṙtī rahīṅ. 6. Agar tum laṙkoṅ ko mana nahīṅ karogē, to woh yahāṅ din bhar shor kartē rahēṅgē. 7. Maiṅ <u>kh</u>ūb jāntā hūṅ keh aur sab ādmī kām kartē rahēṅgē lēkin tum sotē rahogē. 8. Kabhī kabhī woh <u>gh</u>arīb aurat bahut dēr tak roē jātī hai. 9. Agar tum paṙausīoṅ kī murg<u>h</u>īāṅ churā kar khāē jāogē to tum ko bahut sa<u>kh</u>t sazā

milēgī. 10. Hamārā naukar pāgal ādmī kī tarah hañsē jātā hai. 11. Agar tum koshish kīē jāogē to ēk din zarūr kāmyāb hojāogē. 12. Maiñ apnē buḍḍhē naukar ko abhī tak tīs rupai mahīna dīē jātā hūñ. 13. Maiñ apnī musībat kehtā raha aur woh chupkī suntī rahī. 14. Tum apnā kām kīoñ nahīñ kīē jātē ho aur idhar udhar kīā dēkhē jātē ho?

EXERCISE 45(B)

Bullock	Bail	بیل	Grocer	Banyā	بنیا
To rob	Lūṭnā	لوٹنا	Same thing	Ēk hī bāt	ایک ہی بات

1. The villagers go to sleep on their carts, but their bullocks keep going along. 2. The good girls kept on sewing clothes for the soldiers, who continued to fight for their country. 3. The wicked man kept on smiling before the judge. 4. The grocer kept on robbing me for a long time. 5. The dogs kept on barking at the thieves, but they kept on doing their work. 6. What have you been doing? 7. My old servant will keep on sending letters to me. 8. How long will you go on saying the same thing? 9. We kept on watching the enemy from a high hill.

The Uses of the Verbs "DĒKHNĀ"(دیکھنا) "SUNNĀ" (سُننا) AND "PAKARNĀ" (پکڑنا)

Dēkhnā	To see	When these Verbs are used connected with some other Verbs in the same sentence the *Inflected Present Participle* of that Verb is invariably used before them.
Sunnā	To hear	
Pakaṙnā	To catch	

Note :— "Huā", the Inflected Past Participle of "honā" may be used with it.

EXAMPLES

1. I saw the thief running.
   Maiñ nē chor ko dauṙtē dēkhā.

2. She heard the child crying
Us nē bach-chē ko rotē hūē sunā.

3. I never heard him speaking English.
Main nē us ko Aṅgrēzi boltē kabhī nahīṅ sunā.

4. The grocer was caught buying stolen property.
Banyā chorī kā māl kharīdtē hūē pakṙā gāyā.

5. They will arrest him selling your gun.
Who usko tumhārī bandūq bēchtē hūē pakṙēṅgē.

6. We saw the aeroplane flying.
Ham nē hawāī jahāz ko uṙtē dēkhā.

EXERCISE 46(A)

Wada	Promise	وعدہ	Jurmāna جرمانہ	A fine
Qasam	An oath	قسم	Qasam khānā قسم کھانا	To take an oath
Giriftār karnā	To arrest	گرفتار کرنا	Giriftār honā گرفتار ہونا	To be arrested
Ghanṭī *f.*	Bell	گھنٹی	Bandargāh بندرگاہ	Port (Sea)
Ṭikaṭ	Ticket	ٹکٹ	Bajnā بجنا	To be rung; To be sounded
Bajānā بجانا	To sound; to beat; to ring; to play upon, etc.			

1. Maiṅ nē āp usko dīwār mēṅ sūrākh kartē dēkhā. 2. Tum nē dākyē ko bandargāh kī taraf jātē dēkhā? 3. Agar mēm sāheb tum ko bāwarchī khānē kē andar huqqa pītē hūē dēkhēṅgī to tum par jurmāna karēṅgī. 4. Maiṅ nē usko qasam khātē kabhī nahīṅ sunā. 5. Agar tum kisī ādmī ko darakht par chaṙhtē hūē dēkho to usko giriftār karo. 6. Agar laṙkē kabūtaroṅ ko uṙtē hūē

dēkhtē to un par fāir kartē. 7. Agar tum is taraf jāogē to dushman kē jahāz ko dūbtē hūē dēkhogē. 8. Jab unhoṅ nē khānē kī ghanṭī bajtē sunī to woh bhāgtē hūē khānē kē kamrē mēṅ gaē. 9. Mālī nē is ādmī ko sarkārī bāgh mēṅ phūl toṙtē hūē pakṙā. 10. Maiṅ nē is laṙkī ko kaī dafa kahtē sunā kch maiṅ nē apnē khāwind ko wada pūrā kartē kabhī nahīṅ dēkhā. 11. Jab naukar kūttoṅ ko bhauṅktē sunkar apnē gharoṅ sē niklē to unhoṅ nē choroṅ ko bhāgtē dēkhā. 12. Yeh ḍarpok ādmī hamēsha mārtē kē āgē aur bhāgtē kē pīchhē hotā hai.

Official	Sarkārī	سرکاری	Sugar	Shakar	شکر
Canal	Nahṙ	نہر	To carry	Lējānā	لے جانا
To bathe	Nahānā	نہانا			

1. I saw him carrying a gun that day. 2. Who heard my servant saying that? 3. When he saw me coming towards him, he began to run. 4. When I caught the servant stealing wine, I had to send him to the police. 5. Did you yourself hear him say this? 6. Did you see him stop the girl? 7. I saw many men bathing in the canal. 8. Two boys were arrested last night (in the act of) travelling without tickets. 9. The girl will catch the cook stealing sugar. 10. They heard the train coming over the bridge. 11. The officer saw the chaprasī showing the official letter to the people. 12. The General heard his brave soldiers say that they would rather go forward and attack the enemy.

Seasons (*Mausam*) موسم

Winter	Sardī or jāṙā	سردی یا جاڑا	Summer	Garmī	گرمی
Spring	Bahār	بہار	Autumn	Khizāṅ; pat jhaṙ	خزاں پت جھڑ
Rainy season			Barsāt		برسات

Words

Patron	Sarparast	سرپرست	Author	Musannif	مصنّف
Page	Safha	صفحہ	Thumb	Añgūṭhā	انگوٹھا
Mark	Nishān	نشان	Business	Kār-o-bār; kām	کاروبار کام
Field	Khēt	کھیت	Wedding	Shādī *f.*	شادی
Prayer	Namāz	نماز	To seem	Mālūm honā	معلوم ہونا
Accused	Mulzim	ملزم	Already	Pahlē hī	پہلے ہی
To put, to affix	Lagānā	لگانا	Trial	Mushkil, *f.* dushwārī *f.*	مشکل دشوار

REVISIONAL EXERCISE 47(A)

(On Exercises from 38 to 46).

1. The business of patron-finding is one of the trials of authorship. 2. To know whom to write for is to know how to write. 3. We are doing what we can 4. Is there anything on this page you cannot understand? 5. I have explained it to you already. 6. There are many people in the world who cannot do anything themselves, nor do they let any body else do it. 7. Even if they want to do they can't do it. 8. Come near the table; I want to show you something. 9. Each man must put his thumb mark on the receipt of his pay, if he is not able to write his name. 10. If his pay is more than twenty rupees, two one-anna-stamps should be put on the receipt. 11. As I did not let him go to his brother's wedding, he began to cry. 12. You should not have kept a loaded gun in your house. 13. If you cannot come to your work in time you will have to live in the bungalow, and will not be allowed to go home except on Sundays. 14. I allow all my clerks to go for prayers. 15. If you should see the professor, tell him I want to see him. 16. He was to wait for the answer but it seems he has gone away. 17. If you must go, you must. 18. If you will keep on dropping your rifle, you will have to go to the guard room.

19. I used to work in the field. 20. She kept on asking me about her husband, who used to live with me in France. 21. You can take leave now or never. 22. Did you hear me call you? 23. I saw many people come out of the church. 24. The chaukidar says that he often saw the accused speaking to the gardener.

REVISIONAL EXERCISE 47(B)

۱۔ یہ ڈرپوک آدمی ہمیشہ مارتے کے آگے اور بھاگتے کے پیچھے ہوتا ہے۔ ۲۔ جب نوکر کتوں کو بھونکتے سُن کر اپنے گھروں سے نکلے تو انھوں نے چوروں کو بھاگتے دیکھا۔ ۳۔ میں نے آپ کو اس مدرسے میں جاتے ہوئے دیکھا۔ ۴۔ ہم نے ہوائی جہاز اُڑتے ہوئے دیکھا۔ ۵۔ میں نے اس کو اُردو بولتے کبھی نہیں سُنا ۶۔ پٹھان سرحد پر رہتے ہیں۔ ۷۔ اگر تم پڑوسیوں کی مرغیاں چُراتے رہوگے تو تمہارے ہی لیے بُرا ہوگا۔ ۸۔ وہ بیوقوف آدمی ہمیشہ دوسروں کی بات میں دخل دیتا ہے۔ ۹۔ ہم جو کچھ کر سکتے ہیں کر رہے ہیں۔ ۱۰۔ کیا اس خط میں میرے لیے کوئی بات ہے؟ ۱۱۔ دروازے کے قریب آکر یہ چیز لو۔ ۱۲۔ آپ کون ہیں اور کہاں رہتے ہیں؟ ۱۳۔ آپ کے والد (باپ) کا کیا نام ہے؟ ۱۴ آج کل آپ کی والدہ (ماں) کہاں رہتی ہیں؟ کیا وہ آپ کے ساتھ ہیں؟ ۱۵۔ جی ہاں، ہم سب لوگ اکٹھا ہی رہتے ہیں۔ ۱۶۔ جو صبح ہنستے اُٹھتے ہیں وہ سارے دن خوش رہتے ہیں۔ ۱۷۔ اگر تم کو جانا ہی ہے تو پھر چلے جاؤ۔ ۱۸۔ کیا تم نے ریڈیو پر میری تقریر سنی تھی

PART V

USES OF SOME PARTICULAR WORDS

The Uses of "WĀLĀ" (والا)

"Wālā" corresponds exactly with the English words "sort and kind" in the colloquial expression "sort of" and "kind of". It is used in defining or explaining the occupation, habit or characteristics of a living being or inanimate object. For example, "He is a quarrelsome sort of boy" becomes in Urdu "Woh jhagaṙnē wālā laṙkā hai". But, whereas in English the expressions "sort of" and "kind of" are only joined to Adjectives and Participle Adjectives, in Urdu "wālā" can be joined to Nouns or Verbs — or even coupled with a complete phrase. In every case it inflects the words which constitute the definition, explanation, or characterization - provided, of course, that they are susceptible to such inflection. "Wālā" itself agrees with the Noun defined.

The following are examples of its various uses:—

A fighting race	Ēk laṙnē wālī qaum
The nautch girl	Nāchnē wālī laṙkī
A writer	Ēk likhnē wālā (ādmī)
A songstress	Ēk gānē wālī (aurat)
Vendor	Bēchnē wālā
Cloth merchant	Kapṙē wālā
Bookseller	Kitāb wālā
Baker	Roṭī wālā
A two anna-stamp	Do ānē wālā ṭikaṭ
A boy with a long nose	Lambī nāk wālā laṙka

Note:— When joined on to Verbs, "Wālā" may (though it does not always) imply that the action is about to begin. Thus, "ādmī dauṙnē wālā thā" may mean either "the man was a runner" or "the man was just going to run" in such cases the meaning can be gathered from the context.

EXERCISE 48(A)

Gaḍaryā	Shephard	گڈریا	Bhēṛyā	Wolf	بھیڑیا
Watch *n.*	Pahra	پہرہ	Qadam	Pace, step	قدم
Gaz	Yard	گز	Kirāya	Hire, rent	کرایہ
Lāṭhī	Stick	لاٹھی	Pahrē wālā	Sentry; watchman	پہرے والا

1. Tum is anḍē wālē ko jāntē ho? 2. Sāheb ko do bajē wālī gāṛī sē Kohāṭ ko jānā thā, lēkin un ko gāṛī nahīṅ milī. 3. Ṭhanḍē mulkoṅ kē rahnē wālē hamēsha garm kapṛē pahentē haiṅ. 4. Maiṅ Kamishnar sāheb kē sāmnē yeh bāt kahnē wālā thā, keh (when) vakīl sāheb nē mujh ko rokā. 5. Jab tum Rome mēṅ ho, to tum ko Rome wāloṅ kī tarah karnā chāhīē. 6. Bhēṛyā bakrī ko khānē wālā thā, keh gaḍaryē nē usko apnī baṛī lāṭhī sē mār ḍālā. 7. Pahrē wālē sē kaho keh yahāṅ aē. 8. Gāṛī wālē sē pūchho keh tum ko kai ghanṭē kā kirāya chāhīē? 9. Parēd par sab rangrūṭoṅ ko apnē sāmnē wālē ādmī kī pagrī kī taraf dēkhnā chāhīē. 10. Fāyer karnē wālē ādmīoṅ sē pachās qadam pīchhē raho. 11. Dāk k͟hānē jā kar ēk ēk ānē wālē chār ṭikaṭ jaldī sē lao. 12. Tum bahut laṛnē wālē ho. 13. Do bīwīon wālā ādmī kabhī k͟hūsh nahīṅ rahtā hai. 14. Maiṅ āṭh das roz kē wāstē Risālpūr jānē wālā hūṅ. 15. Kenteen wālē ko bulāo. 16. Yeh kālē koṭ wālā ādmī, bangle wale kā naukar hai. 17. Tum mārnē wālē kā hāth pakaṛ saktē ho, magar kahnē wālē kī zabān nahīṅ pakaṛ saktē.

EXERCISE 48(B)

Gold	Sonā	سونا	Silver	Chāṅdī	چاندی
Peace	Aman	امن	Guardian	Muhāfiz	محافظ
To win	Jītnā	جیتنا	To take place	Honā	ہونا
To torment	Satānā	ستانا	To rescue	Bachānā	بچانا
Seldom	Bahut kam	بہت کم			

1. He is penny-cigar smoker. 2. Barking dogs seldom bite. 3. You are a big eater and a great sleeper. 4. She is a very good singer. 5. A great fair is about to take place next week. 6. Tell the fruit seller never to shout when I am asleep. 7. Ten days' leave will be given to all the fighting men. 8. There are many rifle-stealers in this place. 9. I have never seen such a smiling face. 10. The winner will get a gold watch. 14. Who is the sender of this letter? 12. He was about to sign the receipt. 13. The police is the keeper of peace and the guardian of law. 14. My rescuers captured my tormentors at once.

The Uses of "Hī"

"Hī" has no equivalent in English. It is used to give an additional emphasis in the following cases:—

(a) "Hī" is added to the *inflected Present Participle* of a Verb to denote the sense "Immediately after"? as,

On opening—Kholtē hī, On arriving—Pahuňchtē hī.

1. No sooner did he see me, than he ran away.
Mujh ko dēkhtē hī woh bhāg gayā.

2. As soon as the door was opened, all of them entered the room.
Darwāza khultē hī, sab kamrē mēň gaē.

(b) "Hī" is added to Nouns to make them emphatic; as,

1. It is my servant that steals all wine.
Mērā naukar hī sab sharāb churātā hai.

2. Only a camel can move in the sand.
Yeh ūňṭ hī hai, jo rēt mēň chaltā hai.

3. It was the sentry, who broke open the lock of the treasury.
Santary hī nē khazānē kā tālā toṙā.

(c) By adding "I, hī, or hīṅ" equivalent to "very' indeed, the same") the Pronouns and Adverbs are rendered emphatic; as,

Abhī	Just now	ابھی
Kabhī	Ever	کبھی
Tabhī	At that very time	تبھی
Yūṅhī or yūṅhīṅ	In this very way	یونہی یونہیں
Jūṅhī or Jūṅhīṅ	As soon as, No sooner than	جونہی جونہیں
Yahīṅ	In this very place	یہیں
Wahīṅ	In that very place	وہیں
Kahīṅ	Any where	کہیں
Yahīṅ-kahīṅ	Somewhere here	یہیں کہیں
Aur kahīṅ	Somewhere else	اور کہیں
Waisē hī	In that very same manner.	ویسے ہی
Yeh hī or yehī	This same or this very.	یہ ہی ۔ یہی
Woh hī or wohī	That same or that very.	وہ ہی ، وہی

The "h" can be omitted in the oblique cases of the above; as, "Is h ī or اِس ہی isī" اِسی ; "us hī or usī" اُس ہی اُسی

EXAMPLES

This particular man was on my horse.
Yeh hī ādmī mērē ghoṛē par thā.

My brother was in that very room.
Mērā bhāī us hī kamrē mēṅ thā.

He makes a hole in the very plate, off which he eats.
Woh us hī rakābī mēṅ chhēd kartā hai, jis mēṅ khātā hai.

The Uses of the Verb "To have"

The Verb "to have" is used in three different ways:—

(a) As an auxiliary.

(b) To express possession.

(c) In place of other and more definite Verbs.

So far as (a) and (b) are concerned, its place is taken, in Urdu, by "honā"— "to be". In the case of (c) Urdu being a more precise language than English, we use the Verb which gives the exact meaning required. We will examine these in turn:—

1. An auxiliary Verb is one which helps to define the meaning of another Verb. In English "to have" and "to be" are used for the purpose. In Urdu, "to be" and "to go". Compare the following sentences in English and Urdu.

English			*Urdu*
I am falling	*Present*	—	I falling am
I was falling	*Imperfect*	—	I falling was
I have fallen	*Perfect*	—	I fallen am
I had fallen	*Pluperfect*	—	I fallen was
I am sent	*Passive*	—	I sent go

It will be seen that "honā" — (to be) takes the place of "to have."

2. "To have" in the sense of "to possess", also is translated by "honā"

A similar construction is met with in English — e.g. instead of "He has a friend in your office" we can say "There is a friend of his in your office." The latter can be translated almost literally into Urdu; as,

"Uskā ēk dost tumhārē daftar mēn̆ hai"

But in Urdu we have to distinguish between different kinds of possession, for which there are slight differences in construction:—

(a) Those which (as in the example above) take the genitive case with "kā" are as follows:

EXAMPLES

1. The woman has a large garden.
   Aurat kā ēk baṙā bagh hai.

2. My servant has two wives
   Mērē naukar kī do bīwīāṅ haiṅ.

3. He has a long nose :— Uskī lambī nāk hai.

(b) Those which take the genitive case with "kē pās" are all portable or movable possessions- including animals

EXAMPLES

1. He has many books.
   Uskē pās bahut kitābēṅ haiṅ.

2. The English have the largest navy.
   Aṅgrēzoṅ kē pās sab sē baṙā jaṅgī bēṙā hai.

3. I have two horses — Mērē pās do ghoṙē haiṅ.

(c) Those which take the dative case with "ko". These are all abstract things — such as diseases, feelings, habits, opportunity, authority, etc.

EXAMPLES

1. My servant has fever.
   Mērē naukar ko bukhār hai.

2. You have no authority.
   Tum ko kuchh ikhtīār nahīṅ hai.

3. The horse had a bad habit of biting.
Ghořē ko kāṭnē kī kharāb ādat thī.

(d) "To have" is often used loosely in place of other Verbs — e.g. "I am going to have a drink" instead of, "I am to drink a drink".

1. Have a piece of cake — kēk kā ēk ṭukřā khāo
(polite) kēk kā ēk ṭukřā Khā-iyē

2. I want to have a talk with you.
Maiň tumhārē sāth bāt karnā chāhtā hūň.

3. I am going to have a shave.
Maiň hajāmat karūňgā.

EXERCISE 49(A)

Bartan	Utensil	برتن	Sar	Head	سر
Jhanḍā	Flag	جھنڈا	Dāřhī	Beard	داڑھی
Golā bārūd	Ammunition	گولہ بارود	Thūknā	To spit	تھوکنا
kharch	Expenses	خرچ	Hathyār	Arms; weapon	ہتھیار

1. Is gharīb aurat kē pās bartan nahīň haiň. 2. Kiā is lařkī kē māň bāp nahīň haiň? 3. Is ādmī kē pās do ghořē haiň, woh ēk ghořā bēchnā chāhtā hai. 4. Agar tumhārē bēṭī hotī to maiň apnē bēṭē kī shādī us kē sāth kartā. 5. Tumhārē pās bandūq hogī, aur choroň kē pās koī hathyār nahīň hogā, phir unko pakařnā kiā mushkil hai? 6. Shāmī kī lambī dāřhī aur chhoṭā sar thā. 7. Vazīr sāheb kē chapřāsī kā mizāj bahut kharāb hai. 8. Jhaňḍā gāřtē hī dushman kē sab sipāhī bhāgnē lagē. 9. Dushman kē pās na to gola bārūd hai, aur na khānā hai. 10. Agar āj mērē pās rupya hotā to is lařkī sē shādī kartā. 11. Kanjūs ādmī kē pās bahut paisa hai, uskē martē hī us ka bēṭā sab kharch karēgā. 12. Woh afsar hotē hī bahut maghrūr hogayā. 13. Kūēň mēň mat thūko shāyad tum hī

ko is hī mēṅ sē pānī pīnā paṛē. 14. Maiṅ nē do ādmīoṅ kē sāmnē sab rupya jo mērē pās thā usko dīā, aur un hī kē sāmnē us sē rasīd lī.

EXERCISE 49(B)

Relative	Rishtedār	رشتہ دار	Fever	Bu<u>kh</u>ār	بخار
Rank	Darja or Ohda	درجہ/عہدہ	Proud	Ma<u>gh</u>rūr	مغرور
Sorrow	Afsos, <u>gh</u>am	افسوس غم	Pill	Golī	گولی
Master	Mālik	مالک	To rush	Jhapaṭnā	جھپٹنا
Match	Dīā salāī	دیا سلائی	Tail	Dum	دُم
Time to (*spare*)	Fursat	فرصت			

1. Have you got a match? 2. His dog has no tail. 3. My master says, he is sorry, he has no time to see you now. 4. My son has two guns. 5. Have you no warm clothes? 6. This boy has no books. 7. The old woman has no hair. 8. You have no business here. 9. There is no work for you to be here. 10. Has this house two doors? 11. Have you any relative in this city? 12. Who has got fever? 13. I have got your stick. 14. Have you got anything to eat? 15. As soon as the buck saw us, it ran away. 16. As soon as the tiger heard the gun fire, he rushed at me. 17. The poor syce died, soon after he fell off the horse. 18. As soon as he got the higher rank, he became very proud. 19. The gardener begins to do his work, as soon as he comes. 20. His father had his lunch in the dak bungalow. 21. If you have fever, take two pills of quinine.

PART VI

A few narrative stories are given here for translation into Urdu. To enable the students to apply the grammar rules easily, the construction of English used is, as nearly as possible, the same as in Urdu.

The students are advised first to translate a story in writing to be corrected by their Professor. After that, the Professor will tell the same story in his own words, verbally. Then the student should repeat the same story to the Professor.

The above mentioned is meant to exercise both the tongue and the ear, which will, after a short practice, be ready for use to speak and understand respectively.

EXERCISE 50

Recognize	Pahchānnā	پہچاننا	Poet	Shāīr	شاعر
Well-known	Mash-hūr	مشہور	Dissembling	Anjān bankar	انجان بن کر
To copy	Naql karnā	نقل کرنا	To aspire	Kā mushtāq honā	کا مشتاق ہونا
Aid	Madad	مدد	Reputation	Shuhrat	شہرت
Poem	Nazam	نظم	To publish	Shāi karnā	شائع کرنا
Recently	Hāl hī meň	حال ہی میں	To hold out	Phàilānā	پھیلانا

A young man, aspiring to be a poet, used to publish the works of other poets in his name.

Once he copied one of Lord Tennyson's poems, took it to the editor of a wellknown paper, and asked him to be kind enough to publish it, telling him it was a poem which he had recently written.

The editor at once recognised it to be one of Lord Tennyson's poems, but dissembling asked the young poet if he had written the poem unaided. The young man said that he had indeed written every line of it. Hearing this reply the editor rose from his chair, and held out his hand saying; "Then I am very pleased to meet you, Lord Tennyson, I thought you died years ago."

EXERCISE 51

Service	Naukri	نوکری
Order	Tartīb	ترتیب
To appear before	Kē sāmnē pēsh honā	کے سامنے پیش ہونا
Satisfactory	<u>Kh</u>ātir <u>kh</u>wāh	خاطرخواہ
Confident	Itmīnān sē	اطمینان سے
To learn by heart	Zubānī yād karnā	زبانی یاد کرنا

A young recruit was to appear before his commanding officer. As he could not speak English at all, he was very afraid to go before the Colonel. His comrades told him that there was nothing to be afraid of, for the Colonel would ask him only three questions:

(1) "What is your age?"

(2) "How much service have you?"

(3) "Are your rations and pay satisfactory?"

The recruit learnt by heart the answers to the three questions in the same order, and next day confidently went before the Colonel.

It so happened that the Colonel asked the second question first, this is to say:—

"How much service have you?"

"Twenty years," replied the recruit.

"What is your age?" asked the Colonel.

"Six months", was the reply.

Hearing this reply the Colonel said, "My good friend! if that is true, then either you or I must be mad".

"Both sir", was the prompt reply.

EXERCISE 52

Illiterate	An paṛh	ان پڑھ	Railway Station	Isṭēshan	ریلوے اسٹیشن
Loss	Nuqsān	نقصان	Financial	Mālī	مالی
Irate	Ghazabnāk	غضبناک	Booking clerk	Ṭikaṭ Bābū	ٹکٹ بابو
Disappointment	Māyūsī	مایوسی	Arm	Bāzū	بازو
Handle	Dasta	دستہ	To inform	khabar dēnā	خبر دینا
To depart	Rawāna honā	روانہ ہونا	Businessman	Kāro-bārī ādmī or tājir	کاروباری آدمی یا تاجر

Some years ago an illiterate businessman who had to go to a certain city reached the Railway Station just as the train was about to depart. He asked the booking clerk for a ticket, but the latter said "I cannot issue a ticket to you as the train is just going." The businessman said, "Please give me a ticket, I must catch this train, else I shall suffer a great financial loss.

On hearing this the clerk gave him a ticket, and seizing it the businessman rushed off to catch the train. On reaching the train he found it was just starting. The businessman ran up the platform, and managed to get hold of a door handle and stand on the footboard. But to his annoyance a Railway policeman caught him by the arm and pulled him off the train, sayhing to him, "No one is allowed to get into a moving train."

Just then the businessman saw the guard, getting into the guard's van. Off he ran and seizing the guard by the arm, pulled him off. On being asked by the irate guard why he pulled him off, the businessman told him that a Railway policeman had just told him that no one is allowed to get into a moving train.

EXERCISE 53

Tobacco	Tambākū	تمباکو	Breath	Saňs	سانس
Royal	Shāhī	شاہی	Unpleasant	Nāgawār	ناگوار
Jester	Maskharā	مسخرا	Field	Khēt	کھیت
To chew	Chabānā	چبانا	To graze	Charnā	چرنا
To dismiss	Barkhāst karnā	برخواست کرنا	As usual	Māmūl kē mutābiq	معمول کے مطابق
Consequently	Is līe	اس لیے			

A king had a jester, who always used to chew tobacco. Consequently his breath was always very unpleasant. The king did not like this and several times forbade him to chew tobacco, but the jester would not give up this habit. As he was such a good jester, the king did not want to dismiss him.

It so happened that one day the king went out shooting accompanied as usual by his jester. The royal camp was pitched near some tobacco fields. There were some donkeys grazing in those fields, and the king noticed that they only ate the grass, leaving the tobacco alone.

The king at once called for his jester, and pointing to the donkeys said to him, look! even the donkeys do not eat tobacco."

"Your Majesty is quite right, *donkeys* do not eat tobacco", answered the jester smilingly.

EXERCISE 54

Wrath	Ghussa	غصّہ
Blank	Sāda	سادہ
Distinctly	Sāf sāf	صاف صاف
Unforutnately	Badqismatī sē	بدقسمتی سے
Hesitatingly	Ruk ruk kar	رُک رُک کر
Are you quite sure?	Tum ko khūb yaqīn hai?	تم کو خوب یقین ہے ۔

He wondered what to do.	Woh hairān thā keh kīā karē (or) kīā karnā chāhīē. وہ حیران تھا کہ کیا کرے یا کیا کرنا چاہیئے

Mr. Williams gave a letter to his servant and told him to take it to Mr. Smith. The servant took the letter, put it in his pocket; and left for Mr. Smith's bungalow. Now, his pocket being torn, the letter fell out on the way and the servant was not aware of his loss. On reaching Mr. Smith's bungalow he put his hand into his pocket to take out the letter. Being unable to find the letter, and fearing his master's wrath, he was very afraid and started back for the bungalow. Looking for it on the road, along which he had come, he reached his master's bungalow.

Not being able to find the letter, he decided to tell his master that he had lost it, and ask him to write another. Unfortunately the saheb had gone to club. Wondering what he should do about it, he suddenly had a brilliant idea. Going into his master's room he took a piece of blank note paper from the table and put it into an envelope. Having sealed the envelope he rushed off to Mr. Smith's bungalow. As he came in sight of the bungalow, he saw Mr. Smith getting into his car to go to the club.

The servant approaching the saheb made him a very low bow, and handed the letter to him, and stood with his mouth half open, waiting to see what would happen. The saheb finding no name on the envelope asked the servant for whom it was intended. "My master Mr. Williams told me to give it to you, sir", said the servant hesitatingly. Are you quite sure, because there is no name on it", said Mr. Smith. "Yes, sir, I am quite sure it is for you because my master distinctly told me that I was to give it to you personally", said the servant.

Thereupon the saheb said "I think your master must have been in a great hurry to forget to put my name on the envelope". "You are qauite right, sir, he was in a great hurry. This is why he could not write anything inside, either," replied the servant promptly.

INTENSIVE

When a Verb is added to the root of another Verb to give extra force or emphasis to it. it is called an intensive. It is customary even for the uneducated people of India and India to use the intensive forms of the Verb, for by doing so the Verb carries weight and force, and gives full vent to their feelings.

The Intensives are formed by adding to the *unconjugated root* of the principal Verb, the required tense of the following Verbs, which, like an Adverb, or emphatic particle in English, play the chief part in rendering the other Verbs Intensives.

Jānā	To go	جانا	Dēnā	To give	دینا
Paṙnā	To fall	پڑنا	Lēnā	To take	لینا
Uṭhanā	To rise	اُٹھنا	Ḍālnā	To cast down	ڈالنا

No definite rule can be formed to tell which particular intensifying Verb is to be added to a Verb, because different Verbs can be added to the root of the same Verb with different shades of meaning. Therefore, the knowledge of adding the appropriate Verb can only be acquired by careful notice and practice.

Usually the Transitives and Intransitives are added to the Verbs of their respective clauses, with a few exceptions. If either of the two is intransitive, the whole is treated as Intransitive, irrespective of its equivalent in English, and "ne" is not used after the subject in Past Tenses.

Intensives are not used in a negative construction, except in some particular cases.

"Kar" can never be added to any intensive.

Chauňk pařnā	To start up	چونک پڑنا
Jāg uţhnā	To wake up	جاگ اٹھنا
Nikāl dēnā	To turn out	نکال دینا
Pī jānā	To drink up	پی جانا
Khā jānā	To eat up	کھا جانا
Mar jānā	To die	مر جانا
Baiţh jānā	To sit down	بیٹھ جانا
So jānā	To fall asleep	سو جانا
Chalā jānā	To go away	چلا جانا
Ā jānā	To come away, To turn up	آ جانا
Bol pařnā	To speak up	بول پڑنا
Bol uţhnā	*abruptly*	بول اٹھنا
Rakh lēnā	To lay by	رکھ لینا
Rakh dēnā	To set down	رکھ دینا
Mār d̄ālnā	To kill outright	مار ڈالنا
Kāţ d̄ālnā	To cut down	کاٹ ڈالنا
Phēňk dēnā	To throw away	پھینک دینا
Ro pařnā	To burst into tears	رو پڑنا
Kūd pařnā	To jump down	کود پڑنا
Pařh d̄ālnā	To read off	پڑھ ڈالنا
Ho jānā	To become, To be completed	ہو جانا
D̄āl dēnā	To throw down, To cast down	ڈال دینا
Haňs dēnā	To laugh *to enjoy*	ہنس دینا
Samajh jānā	To understand	سمجھ جانا
Haňs dēnā	To laugh *undisguisedly*	ہنس دینا
Haňs pařnā	To laugh *involuntarily*	ہنس پڑنا

Kah ḍālnā	To speak out *undisguisedly*	کہہ ڈالنا
Gir jānā	To fall down *accidentally*	گر جانا
Kah dēnā	To tell	کہہ دینا
Uṙā dēnā	To blow up	اُڑا دینا
Gir paṙnā	To fall down *suddenly*	گر پڑنا
Chal paṙnā	To start off *suddenly*	چل پڑنا
Toṙ dēnā	To break up*accidentaly*	توڑ دینا
Toṙ ḍālnā	To break up *intentionally*	توڑ ڈالنا
Tūṭ jānā	To be broken *accidentaly*	ٹوٹ جانا
Phāṙ denā	To tear up	پھاڑ دینا
Phāṙ ḍālnā	To tear up *rashly*	پھاڑ ڈالنا
Dē-dēnā	To hand over	دے دینا
Dē-dēnā	To give away *Indiscriminately*	دے دینا
Lē-lēnā	To take hold of; to seize	لے لینا

The following examples will show the force of the different intensifying Verbs:—

JANA جانا

Jānā جانا is added to show *completion*; as,

Top chal gaī hai aur bāra baj gaē haiṅ. Chapṙāsī baiṅk sē wāpas ā gayā hai. Daftar kā sab kām hogayā hai aur kāghazoṅ par dastkhat hogaē haiṅ. Sab afsar mess ko chalē gaē haiṅ aur khānā khānē kē līē mēz par baiṭh gaē haiṅ. Darwāzē kē sāmnē sē hat jāo aur ēk taraf baiṭh jāo. Agar mērē hāth sē koī chīz gir jāēgī to ṭūṭ jāēgī, sāheb khafā hojāēṅgē. Ēk ghantē kē bād tumhārī chiṭ-ṭhī sāheb kē pās pahuṅch jāēgī aur tum ko jawāb mil jāēgā.

(پڑنا)

Paṙnā پڑنا and uṭhnā اُٹھنا show *suddenness* and *surprise*; as,

Ēk rāt ko kuchh dākū ēk baṅglē mēṅ ghus paṛē, ēk dākū kī bandūq ēkā ēkī chal paṛī. Uskī āwāz sē sāheb jāg uṭhā aur uskī bīwī chauṅk paṛī. Sab naukar ghabrā kar kamrē kī taraf dauṛ paṛē. Bhāgtē bhāgtē ēk dākū gir paṛā, chaukīdār bol uṭhā keh kaun hai? Ḍākū nē us kī taraf bandūq chhatyāī to bēchārā kāṅp uṭhā aur ro paṛā. Bahādur chaukīdār ko rotē dēkh kar ḍākū haṅs paṛā.

(ڈالنا)

Ḍālnā ڈالنا shows *force, rashness, or indiscretion*, as,

Ēk chor nē ēk kamrē kā darwāza toṛ dālā aur andar jā kar sab sē pahlē tēlīfūn kā tār kāṭ dālā. Jab kuttā bhauṅkā to us ko mār ḍālā. Bahut kāghaz phāṛ ḍālē aur naqdī lēkar sīdhā sharāb khānē ko chalā gayā. Wahāṅ pahuṅch kar kaī rupai kī sharāb pī ḍālī. Nashē kī hālat mēṅ bāqī rupai dostoṅ ko dē ḍālē aur chorī kā sab hāl shurū sē akhir tak kah ḍālā.

"DĒNĀ" دینا

Dēnā دینا is added when a person does anything for the benefit, comfort, or interest of anyone else.

"LĒNĀ" لینا

Lēnā is added when a person does anything for his own interest or credit.

WORDS

Hāl	Account	حال
Shurū sē	From the beginning	شروع سے
Shurū karnā	To begin	شروع کرنا
Sīdhā	Straight	سیدھا
Bāqī	Remaining	باقی
Nasha	Intoxication	نشہ

Ēkā ēkī	All of a sudden	یکایکی
Āwāz	Voice; sound, noise.	آواز
Hālat	State	حالت
Naqdī	Cash	نقدی
Ā<u>kh</u>ir	End	آخر
Ā<u>kh</u>ir tak	To the end	آخر تک
Kaṅpnā	To tremble	کانپنا
Bechāra	Poor fellow	بے چارہ
Chhatyānā	To level a gun	چھتیانا
Ghabrānā	To be alarmed	گھبرانا
Sharāb <u>kh</u>āna	Tavern; bar	شراب خانہ
Ghusnā	To force one's way in	گھسنا

EXAMPLES

1. Santarī nē afsar kē wāstē darwāza khol diā.
The sentry opened the door for the officer.
سنتری نے افسر کے واسطے دروازہ کھول دیا

2. Mālum nahīṅ keh chor nē darwāza kaisē khol liā.
I wonder how the thief managed to open the door.
معلوم نہیں چور نے دروازہ کیسے کھول دیا

3. Ham nē tumhārī tan<u>kh</u>wāh mālī ko dē-dī hai, us sē māṅg lo (or lē-lo). ہم نے تمہاری تنخواہ مالی کو دے دی ہے اس سے مانگ لو یا لے لو
I have given your pay to the gardener, ask him for it.

4. Lo, yeh do rupai haiṅ, ēk rupiā tum lē-lo aur ēk <u>kh</u>idmatgār ko dē-do.
Here are two rupees, you take one, and give one to the <u>kh</u>idmatgār (servant).
لو یہ دو روپے ہیں۔ ایک تم لے لو اور ایک خدمت گار کو دیدو

RĒL KĀ SAFAR (*Railway Journey*)

Sāheb — Dēkho bearer, āj rāt ham Gorakhpūr jāeṅgē, hamārā safar kā sāmān ṭhīk karo.

Bearer — Bahut ach-chhā, janāb, kaunsī gāṛī sē jāeṅgē? (or) gāṛī kai bajē jātī hai?

Sāheb — Gāṛī ēk bajē rawāna hotī hai (*or*) chhūṭtī hai. Tāṅgē wālē sē kah-do* keh ṭhīk bāra bajē tāṅgā yahāṅ lāē, dēr na karē.

Bearer — Janāb khātir jama rakhēṅ, dēr nahīṅ hogī.

(Bara Baje)

Bearer — Janāb tāṅgā a gayā hai.

Sāheb — Ach-chhā tum sāmān tāṅgē par lādo. Dēkho gin lo kitnē banḍal haiṅ; aur koī chīz bhūlnā nahīṅ.

Bearer — Janāb maiṅ nē sab sāmān shām ko bāṅdh kar alag ēk konē mēṅ rakh diā thā.

Sāheb — (Tāṅgē wālē sē) Ham ko dēr hogaī hai, tāṅgā tēz chalāo. Dēkho ham gāṛī sē rah na jāēṅ.

Tāṅgē-wala— Janāb, ap fikr na karēṅ, mērā ghoṛā hawā kī tarah tēz chaltā hai. Maiṅ āp ko pāṅch minaṭ mēṅ isṭēshan par pahuṅchā dūṅgā.

(Isteshan par pahunch kar)

Sāheb — (Tāṅgē wālē sē) Kitnā kirāya hūā?

Tāṅgē-wala— Janāb bārah ānē hūē.

Sāheb — Ach-chhā lo yeh ēk rupīa hai. Hamārī taraf sē tum chār ānē kī miṭhāī khā-lēnā.

---

* Read the preceding rule about the Intensives.

Sāheb — (Bearer se) Dēkho maiň to ţikaţ khārīdnē jātā hūň, tum jākar daryāft karo keh gāřī kaunsē plaţform sē jātī hai, aur sab sāmān qulion par wahāň lējāo.

Sāheb — (Ţikaţ Bābū se) Mehrbānī sē mujhē Gorakhpūr kā ēk awwal darjē kā, aur ēk naukar kē wāstē tīsrē darjē kā ţikaţ jaldī sē dē-do. Gāřī kē jānē mēň kitnī dēr hai?

Bābū — Āp ghabrāēň nahīň, gāřī kē jānē mēň abhī das minaţ bāqī haiň.

Sāheb — Donoň ţikţon kē kiā dām hūē.

Bābū — Bāsaţh rupai tīn ānē.

Sāheb — Hamārē pās sau rupai kā noţ hai, āp kē pās bāqī hai?

Bābū — Jī hāň hai, yeh saiňtīs rupai tēra ānē lījīe.

(Gāřī mēň sawār ho kar)

Sāheb — (Bearer sē) Qūlīoň ko mazdūrī dēkar jaldī sē hamārā bistar kar-do.

Bearer — Janāb bistar taīyār hai, kuchh aur hukm hai?

Sāheb — Ham ko nāshta kal subah chhē bajē chāhīē.

Bearer — Janāb aur kuchh?

Sāheb — Nahīň aur kuchh nahīň, bas.

(Subah ko chhe bajē)

Bearer — Janāb nāshta taīyār hai.

Sāheb — Ach-chhā rakh do. Dēkho bhūlnā nahīň, ham ko Kānpūr mēň gāřī badalnī hai. Wahāň ham kis waqt pahuňchēňgē?

Bearer — Koī tīň bajkar bīs minaţ par.

(Kānpūr kē isṭēshan par)

Gāṙī isṭēshan par pahuṅchtī hai, magar bearer kā kuchh pata nahīṅ. Sāheb gāṙī sē utartē haiṅ aur qulī gāṙī sē asbāb utārnā shurū kartē haiṅ keh itnē mēṅ bearer bhī sāmnē sē ātā hai.

Sāheb — (Khafā hokar) Bearer, jaldī karo, itnī dēr kahān rahē.

Bearer — (Rotī āwāz sē) Janāb kisī nē mērī jūtīāṅ churā lī haiṅ, un ko ḍhūnḍ rahā thā.

Sāheb — (Haṅs kar) Khair fikr nā karo aglī gāṙī mēṅ tum bhī kisī aur ādmī kī jūtīān churā lēnā. Dēkho sāmān tāṅgē mēṅ rakho, aur tāṅgē wālē sē kaho keh O. & R. istēshan ko chalē.

(O. & R. isṭēshan par)

Sāheb — (Bearer sē) Dēkho maiṅ to kuchh khānā khānē kē wāstē jātā hūṅ, aur tum yeh daryāft kar lo keh gāṙī kai bajē jātī hai?

Bearer — Janāb rāt ko paunē das bajē.

Sāheb — Tum sē kis nē kahā?

Bearer — Janāb qulī nē.

Sāheb — Qulī ko is kī kiā khabar? Jākar isṭēshan māsṭer sāheb sē pūchho.

Bearer — Janāb, isṭēshan māsṭar sāheb kahtē haiṅ kēh āj sē gāṙī kā waqt badal gayā hai, sāṙhē sāt bajē jāēgī.

Sāheb — Tum nē dēkhā, agar ham qulī kē kahnē par rahtē to rāt bhar isṭēshan par paṙā rahnā paṙtā.

(Kānpūr sē rawāngī)

Sāheb — Yeh gāṛī subha āṭh bajē Gorakhpūr pahuṅchēgī, wahāṅ pahuṅchtē hī qulīoṅ ko bulā kar hamārā sāmān awwal darjē kē wēṭing rūm mēṅ lējānā.

Bearer — Bahut ach-chhā, janāb.

(Gorakhpūr pahuṅch kar)

Sāheb — Khidmatgār sē keh do keh maiṅ ēk ghanṭē mēṅ nāshta karūṅgā. Us sē kah kar mērā hajāmat kā sāmān aur safēd sūṭ baks mēṅ sē nikāl do.

(Kapṛē pahennē kē bād)

Sāheb — Nāshta taīyār hai?

Bearer — Jī hāṅ, taīyār hai.

Sāheb — (Wēṭar sē) Menū kahāṅ hai?

Waiter — Janāb abhī lātā hūṅ.

Sāheb — (Gosht kī taraf ishāra kar kē) yeh kiā hai?

Waiter — Janāb, gosht hai.

Sāheb — Kiā gosht aisā hī hotā hai? Is ko kaun chabā saktā hai? Is ko lējāo, jaldī sē kuchh aur lāo. Magar khudā kē wāstē is dafa ādmīon kē khānē kī kuchh chīz lānā.

(Nāshtē kē bād)

Sāheb — (Bearer sē) - Ēk ṭaxī lāo, aur yeh bhī daryāft karo keh yahāṅ kirāya kis hisāb sē lētē haiṅ?

Bearer — Janāb taxī ā gaī hai. Pahlē ghanṭē kā kirāya bāra ānē aur bād mēṅ chhe ānē fī ghanṭā. Yeh sarkārī nirkh hai.

Sāheb — (Taxī wālē sē) Sēnṭral Hoṭal ko chalo.

THE NUMERALS

1	Ēk	ایک	27	Sat-tāīs	ستائیس
2	Do	دو	28	Aṭ-ṭhāīs	اٹھائیس
3	Tīn	تین	29	Unat-tīs	انتیس
4	Chār	چار	30	Tīs	تیس
5	Pāňch	پانچ	31	Ikat-tīs	اکتیس
6	Chhe	چھ	32	Bat-tīs	بتیس
7	Sāt	سات	33	Tēňtīs	تینتیس
8	Āṭh	آٹھ	34	Chauňtīs	چونتیس
9	Nau	نو	35	Paiňtīs	پینتیس
10	Das	دس	36	Chhat-tīs	چھتیس
11	Gīāra	گیارہ	37	Saiňtīs	سینتیس
12	Bāra	بارہ	38	Ařtīs	اڑتیس
13	Tēra	تیرہ	39	Untālīs	اُنتالیس
14	Chauda	چودہ	40	Chālīs	چالیس
15	Pandra	پندرہ	41	Iktālīs	اکتالیس
16	Sola	سولہ	42	Bayālīs	بیالیس
17	Satra	سترہ	43	Tēňtālīs	تینتالیس
18	Aṭṭhāra	اٹھارہ	44	Chawālīs	چوالیس
19	Unnīs	اُنیس	45	Paiňtālīs	پینتالیس
20	Bīs	بیس	46	Chhīālīs	چھیالیس
21	Ik-kīs	اکیس	47	Saiňtālīs	سینتالیس
22	Bāīs	بائیس	48	Ařtālīs	اڑتالیس
23	Tēīs	تیئیس	49	Unanchās	اُنچاس
24	Chaubīs	چوبیس	50	Pachās	پچاس
25	Pach-chīs	پچیس	51	Ik-kīāwan	اکیاون
26	Chhab-bīs	چھبیس	52	Bāwan	باون

53	Tirēpan	ترپن	80	Assī	اسّی
54	Chaw-wan	چوّن	81	Ik-kīāsī	اکیاسی
55	Pachpan	پچپن	82	Bayāsī	بیاسی
56	Chhap-pan	چھپن	83	Tirāsī	تراسی
57	Sat-tāwan	ستاون	84	Chaurāsī	چوراسی
58	Aṭ-ṭhāwan	اٹھاون	85	Pich-chāsī	پچاسی
59	Uṅsaṭh	اُنسٹھ	86	Chhiāsī	چھیاسی
60	Sāṭh	ساٹھ	87	Sat-tāsī	ستاسی
61	Iksaṭh	اکسٹھ	88	Aṭ-ṭhāsī	اٹھاسی
62	Bāsaṭh	باسٹھ	89	Nawāsī	نواسی
63	Tirēsaṭh	ترسٹھ	90	Nawwē	نوّے
64	Chauṅsaṭh	چونسٹھ	91	Ik-kānwē	اکیانوے
65	Paiṅsaṭh	پینسٹھ	92	Bānwē	بانوے
66	Chhīāsaṭh	چھیاسٹھ	93	Tirānwē	ترانوے
67	Saṙsaṭh	سڑسٹھ	94	Chaurānwē	چورانوے
68	Aṙsaṭh	اڑسٹھ	95	Pich-chānwē	پچانوے
69	Unhat-tar	اُنہتر	96	Chhīānwē	چھیانوے
70	Sat-tar	ستّر	97	Sat-tānwē	ستانوے
71	Ikhat-tar	اکہتر	98	Aṭ-ṭhānwē	اٹھانوے
72	Bahat-tar	بہتر	99	Nin-nānwē	ننّانوے
73	Tehat-tar	تہتّر	100	Saū	سَو
74	Chauhat-tar	چوہتر	500	Pāṅch sau	پانچ سَو
75	Pichhat-tar	پچھتر	1,000	Ēk hazār	ایک ہزار
76	Chhiat-tar	چھہتر	100,000	Ēk lākh	ایک لاکھ
77	Sathat-tar	ستہتر	1,000,000	Das lākh	دس لاکھ
78	Aṭhat-tar	اٹھہتر	10,000,000	Ēk karoṙ	ایک کروڑ
79	Unāsī	اُناسی			

Other numbers are expressed thus:—

112	—	Ēk sau bāra (or) ēk sau aur bāra
1,250	—	Ēk hazār do sau pachās (or) bāra sau pachās
1,916	—	Ēk hazār nau sau sola (or) unnīs sau sola
1,12,310	—	Ēk lākh, bāra hazār, tīn̆ sau das

The Ordinals

(Or the numbers showing the order)

The first six numbers (except the 5th) are irregular, but from the 7th upwards they are formed regularly by adding "wan" to any number; as,

1st	Pahlā	پہلا	4th	Chauthā	چوتھا
2nd	Dūsrā	دوسرا	5th	Pān̆chwān̆	پانچواں
3rd	Tīsrā	تیسرا	6th	Chhaṭā	چھٹا

From 7th upwards they are formed regularly by adding "wān̆" as 20th— Bīswān̆; 55th — Pachpanwān̆.

Note:— The "ā" of "w ān̆" is subject to change according to the Number and Gender of the following Noun; as,

1.	The first room	—	Pahlā kamra	پہلا کمرہ
2.	The seventh boy	—	Sātwān̆ laṙkā	ساتواں لڑکا
3.	On the tenth horse	—	Daswēn̆ ghoṙē par	دسویں گھوڑے پر
4.	The fifth girl	—	Pān̆chwīn̆ laṙkī	پانچویں لڑکی

(a) When the fractions are used *alone*, they are expressed thus:—

¼ -pāo پاؤ ½ - ādhā آدھا ¾ - paunā پونا

Quarter of an hour	—	Pāo ghanṭa	پاؤگھنٹہ
Half an hour	—	Ādhā ghanṭa	آدھا گھنٹہ
Three quarter of an hour	—	Paunā ghanṭa	پونا گھنٹہ

(b) The compound fractions are formed by adding to the required number :—

"Sawā" and a quarter; سوا	"Sāṙhē" and a half; ساڑھے
"Paunē" quarter less than. پونا	

Note : — Only the compound fractions 1½ and 2½ are irregular and have special words to denote them, all the others are regular; as,

1¼	—	Sawā	3 ¾	—	Paunē chār
1 ½	—	Dēṙh (*irregular*)	4 ¼	—	Sawā chār
1 ¾	—	Paunē do	4 ½	—	Sāṙhē chār
2¼	—	Sawā do	4 ¾	—	Paunē pāṅch
2 ½	—	Dhāī (*irregular*)	5 ¼	—	Sawā pāṅch
2 ¾	—	Paunē tīn	5 ½	—	Sāṙhē pāṅch
3 ¼	—	Sawā tīn	5 ¾	—	Paunē chhe
3 ½	—	Sāṙhē tīn	6 ½	—	Sāṙhē chhe

Totality or universality is expressed by adding "oṅ" to the ordinary Number, as,

Both	Donoṅ	دونوں	All the three	Tīnoṅ	تینوں
All the seven	Sātoṅ	ساتوں	All the fifty	Pachāsoṅ	پچاسوں

Bring both the horses here,
Donoṅ ghoṙoṅ ko yahāṅ lāo. دونوں گھوڑوں کو یہاں لاؤ

I have four servants, and all the four of them are lazy.
Mērē chār naukar haiṅ, aur chāroṅ sust haiṅ.
میرے چار نوکر ہیں اور چاروں سست ہیں ۔

The Multiplicatives are formed by adding the word "gunā" — (*fold*) to a cardinal number; as,

Do gunā or Dugnā	—	Twofold	دوگنا یا دُگنا
Tīn gunā or Tignā	—	Threefold	تین گنا یا تِگنا
Das gunā	—	Tenfold	دس گنا
Pandra gunā	—	Fifteenfold	پندرہ گنا

PART VII

Useful Sentences

(1) Food

1. Get my dinner quickly — Mērā khānā jaldī lāo.

2. Look here, this spoon is not clean.
   Dēkho, yeh chamcha sāf nahīn̆ hai.

3. This meat is under done — Yeh gosht kach-chā hai.

4. This potato is over-cooked. — Yeh ālū bahut gal gayā hai.

5. What fruits are there in the bazaar? — Bāzār mēn̆ kīā kīā mēwā hai?

6. This cup is broken — Yeh pīālā tūṭā hūā hai.

7. No sir, it is not broken — Nahīn̆ sāheb sābut hai.

8. Sharpen this knife quickly, — Yeh chhurī jaldī tēz karo.

9. Always bring fresh fish Hamēsha tāzī machhlī lāo.

10. This bread is stale — Yeh roṭī bāsī hai.

11. Take away the tea tray — Chāē kī ṭarē lējāo.

12. Clean your hands — Apnē hāth sāf karo.

13. Don't put your finger inside the cup. — Pīālī mēn̆ ūn̆glī mat ḍālo.

14. Throw this soup away — Yeh shorbā phēnkdo.

15. Look here, it smells — Dēkho is mēn̆ bū ātī hai.

16. Bring some boiling water. — Thoṙā khaultā pāni lāo.

17. Put some more ice in it. — Is mēṅ thoṙī baraf aur ḍālo.

18. I shall dine out tonight. — Āj shām ko mērā khānā bāhar hai.

19. This meat is bad — Yeh gosht saṙā hūā hai.

20. Bring breakfast quickly — Nāshta jaldī lāo.

21. This cheese smells — Is panīr mēṅ bū hāi.

22. Don't butter the toast — Tos par makkhan mat lagāo.

23. Bring some pepper and salt. — Thoṙā namak aur gol mirch lāo.

24. I don't like ghi — Mujh ko ghī pasand nahīṅ hai.

25. This orange is very sour. — Yeh saṅgtara bahut khaṭṭā hai.

26. This mango is very sweet — Yeh ām bahut mīṭhā hai.

27. This banana is very delicious. — Yeh kēlā bahut mazēdār hai.

28. The monkeynuts are bitter. — Mūṅg phalīāṅ kaṙwī haiṅ.

29. This is very tasteless. — Yeh bahut be maza hai.

30. Is this biscuit dry or sweet? — Yeh biskuṭ namkīn hai yā mīṭhā hai.

31. What time do you want tea, sir?—Janāb ko chāē kitnē bajē chāhīē?

32. I want tea at quarter to five.— Mujh ko chāē paunē pāṅch bajē chāhīē.

(2) TIME

1.	What time is it ?	—	Kīā waqt hai ?
2.	It is one o'clock	—	Ēk bajā hai.
3.	It is two o'clock	—	Do bajē haiň.
4.	Quarter past one	—	Sawā bajē (not sawā ēk).
5.	Half past one	—	Ḍeṙh bajē (not sāṙhē ēk)
6.	Half past two	—	Ḍhāī bajē (not sāṙhē do)
7.	Quarter to three	—	Paunē tīn bajē.
8.	Quarter past three	—	Sawā tīn bajē.
9.	Half past three	—	Sāṙhē tīn bajē.
10.	Quarter to four	—	Paunē chār bajē.

11. It is ten minutes to four.
    Chār bajnē mēň das minaṭ (kam or bāqī) haiň.
    or Das minaṭ kam chār bajē haiň.

12. It is ten minutes past four.
    Chār bajkar das minaṭ hūē haiň.

13. Are you free (or) can you spare time?
    Tum ko fursat hai?

14.	I am very busy	—	Mujh ko bahut kām hai.
15.	I have no time to spare	—	Mujh ko fursat nahīň hai.
16.	Be here in time	—	Waqt par ānā.
17.	Don't be long	—	Dēr mat karnā.

18. How long ago?
    (*If a matter of hours or minutes*) kitnī dēr hūī
    (*If a matter of month or days*) kitnē din (or roz) hūē.

19. How long will you wait here?
Tum yahāň *kitnē din* thairogē.

20. How long will you stay at Bombay?
Tum Bombay mēň kitnē din (or roz) ţhairogē?

21. This clock is ten minutes slow.
Yeh ghanţa das minaţ pīchhē hai.

22. My watch is ten minutes fast.,
Mērī ghařī das minaţ āgē hai.

23. You are late — Tum dēr sē āē ho.

24. You are early — Tum waqt sē pahlē āē ho.

25. You never do any thing in time.
Tum koi kām waqt par nahīň kartē ho.

26. Get it ready by Saturday.
Is ko haftē tak taīyār karo.

27. Have you got the watch with you?
Tumhārē pās ghařī hai?

28. I shall be back in a minute.
Main abhī wāpas ātā hūn.

29. How long will you take to make it?
Tum is ko kitnī dēr mēň banāogē?

Miscellaneous Sentences

1. Is any one there ? — Koī (ādmī) hai?
2. Come on, hurry up — Chalo, jaldī karo.
3. Go away — Chalē jāo.
4. Get out of the way — Haţ jāo.
5. Keep to the left — Bāēň hāth ko chalo.

6.	Look to your front	—	Sāmnē dēkho.
7.	Get back	—	Pīchhē haṭo.
8.	Wait a little	—	Zara ṭhairo.
9.	Keep straight on	—	Sīdhē chalē jāo.
10.	Turn to your right	—	Dāēñ hāth ko ghūmo.
11.	Turn to your left	—	Bāēñ hāth ko ghūmo.
12.	Where have you been?	—	Tum kahāñ thē.
13.	Ask the manager	—	Manījar sē pūchho.
14.	Is the English Mail in	—	Iñglistān kī ḍāk ā gaī?
15.	Are you drunk?	—	Tum nashē mēñ ho?
16.	Keep awake	—	Hoshyār raho, *or* so mat
17.	Watch the ball	—	Gaind ko dēkhtē raho.
18.	Thank you	—	Āp kī mehrbānī hai.
19.	Please yourself	—	Jaisī tumhārī khūshī.
20.	Whom are you after ?	—	Kisko dēkhtē ho?
21.	What do you want ?	—	(Tum ko) kīā chāhīē?
22.	Where do you live?	—	Tumhārā ghar kahāñ hai?

23. Which is the right way to the cantonment?

Chhāonī ko sīdhā rāstā kaunsā hai?

24.	How old are you ?	—	Tumhārī umr kīā hai ?
25.	What did he say ?	—	Usnē kīā kahā?
26.	Remind me tomorrow	—	Mujh ko kal yād dilāo.
27.	Do not speak so fast	—	Itnī jaldī mat bolo.
28.	What do you mean?	—	Tumhārā kīā matlab hai.
29.	Do you understand	—	Tum samajhtē ho?
30.	I do not understand you	—	Main tumhārī bāt nahīñ samajhta.
31.	I do not believe you.	—	Main tumhārī bāt nahīñ māntā.

32.	I trust you	—	Mujh ko tumhārā etbār hai.
33.	I am sure	—	Mujh ko yaqīn hai.
34.	I don't know	—	Mujh ko mālūm nahīn̆.
35.	I am right	—	Mērī bāt thīk hai.
36.	You are wrong	—	Tumhārī bāt ghalat haī.
37.	Don't be afraid	—	Ḍaro mat.
38.	Don't make a fool of me.	—	Mujh ko bēwaqūf mat banāo.
39.	Don't bother me	—	Mujh ko diq mat karo.
40.	Alright, leave it alone	—	Ach-chhā is ko rahnē do.
41.	Never mind	—	Kuchh parwā nahīn̆.
42.	Go and mind your own business	—	Jāo, apnā kām karo.
43.	Is there any answer to it ?	—	Is kā kuchh jawāb hai?
44.	No, there is no answer to it	—	Nahīn̆ is kā kuchh jawāb nahīn̆ hai.
45.	Put an anna stamp on it.	—	Is par ēk ānē kā ṭikaṭ lagāo.
46.	Post this letter	—	Yeh chiṭṭhī ḋāk mēn̆ dālo.
47.	What's up	—	Kīā hūā.
48.	Don't shout	—	Chillāo mat
49.	Shut up or be quiet	—	Chup raho.
50.	Don't chatter	—	Bak bak mat karo.
51.	It is useless	—	Yeh bē-fāida hai.
52.	I shall ride (a horse)	—	Main̆ ghoṙē par jāon̆gā.
53.	I shall drive	—	Main̆ gāṙī chalaon̆gā.
54.	I shall go by car	—	Main̆ moṭor mēn̆ jāon̆gā.
55.	I shall walk	—	Main̆ paidal jāon̆gā.

56. Can a man go there on a bicycle?

Kia wahān̆ ēk ādmī bāīsīcal par jā saktaī hai.

57.	Is the road fit for driving ?	—	Gāṙī chalane kā rāsta thīk hai?
58.	Do you know Persian ?	—	Tum Fārsī jāntē ho?

59. Is there any one here who can speak Urdu?
    Yahāň koī Urdu bolnē wālā ādmī hai?
60. Can we get any milk in the village?
    Gāoň mēň dūdh mil saktā hai?
61. Tell the nambardar I want him — Nambardar ko bulao (or)
    Nambardār sē kaho kēh sāheb būlatē haiň.
62. What do I owe you ?
    Mujh par tumhārā kitnā paisa chāhīē?
63. He owes me ten rupees. — Us par mērē das rupai chāhīēň
64. It appears — Aisā mālūm hotā hai
65. Nabbu seems to be very honest.
    Nabbū bahut īmāndār mālūm hotā hai.
66. This seems to be a good book.
    Yeh achchhī kitāb mālūm hotī hai.
67. There is one rupee too many. — Ēk rupīa zīada hai.
68. There is one anna short. — Ēk āna kam hai.
69. I like you for it.
    Mujh ko tumhārī yeh bāt pasand hai.
70. Get that man out of my sight.
    Us ādmī ko mērē sāmnē sē haṭā do.
71. Why don't you speak, when you are spoken?
    Jab koī bolē to jawāb kioň nahīň dētē ho?
72. It comes to the same thing. — Yeh ēk hī bāt hai.
73. I cannot get my tongue round this word.
    Yeh lafz mērī zabān par nahīň chaṛhtā.
74. But me not buts. — Mujh sē agar magar mat karo.

PART VIII

(VOCABULARY)

(ENGLISH—URDU)

ABBREVIATIONS

m. — Masculine, *f.* Feminine, *adj.* Adjective, *adv.* Adverb, *c.* Conjunction *In.* Interjection. *Pro.* Pronoun, *Pre.* Preposition, *v. tr.*—Verb Transitive *v. Int.* Verb Intransitive *k.* karna; *h* hona; *d.* dena; *j.* jana.

A

Abandon	Chhoř dēnā
Ability	Liāqat *f.*
Able *adj.*	Lāiq.
Abode	Thikāna *m.*
Abolish	Mauqūf karnā
Abound	Kasrat sē honā
About (nearly)	Taqrīban
About (*Concerning*)	kī bābat
Above	Kē ūpar.
Abreast	Barābar
Abroad	Pardēs *m.*
Abruptly *adv.*	Ēkā ēkī.
Absent *adj.*	Ghair hāzīr
Absence *adj.*	Ghair hāzirī
Absolute *adj.*	Mutlaq
Absurd *adj.*	Bēhūda
Abundance	Kasrat *f.*
Abundant	Bahut.
Abuse	Gālī *f.*
Abuse *v. tr.*	Gālī dēnā.,
Accept	Qabūl karnā
Access	Pahuňch *f.*
Accident	Hādisā *m.*
Accordingly	Chunāňcheh.
According to	Kē muāfiq
Accurate	Ţhīk
Accuasation	Ilzām *m.*
Accuse	(par) ilzām lagānā
Accused	Mulzim
Across	Kē pār
Active	Chālāk
Actual *adj.*	Asl
Address	Pata

Admiration	Tarif *f.*
Admonish to	Tanbih *k.*
Advance (money)	Peshgi *f.*
Advance	Āgē bařhnā
Advance guard	Harāwal
Advantage	Fāeda *m.*
Advice	Salāh *f.*
Advisable	Munāsib
Aerial	Hawāī
Affair	Muāmla *m.*
Affection	Muhab-bat *f.*
Afraid, to be	D̄arnā
After	Kē bād
Again	Phīr
Against	Kē <u>Kh</u>ilāf
Agitate	Ubhārnā *v. tr.*
Ago	Hūā
Agree	(Par) rāzī honā
Agreement	Iqrār Nāma
Agriculture	Kāshtkārī *f.* or Zirā'at *f.*
Agriculturist	Kāshtkār
Ague	Jāřē kā bu<u>kh</u>ār *m.*
Ahead	Āgē
Aid	Madad
Air	Hawā
Aim	Nishāna *m.*
Air *adj.*	Hawāī
Airship	Hawāī jahāz *m.*
Air raid	Hawāī hamla
Alight	Utarnā *v. Int.*
Alike	Yaksāň
Alive	Zinda
All	Sab
Ally	Dost *m.*
Almond	Bādām *m.*
Almost	Qarīb qarīb
Alms	<u>Kh</u>airāt *f.*
Alone	Akēlā
Already	Pahlē hī
Also	Bhī
Alter	Badalnā
Although	Agarcheh
Always	Hamesha
Ambulance	Bimaroň kī Gāřī
Ambush	Ghāt
Ammunition	Gola bārūd
Amusing	Dilchasp
Anchor	Laňgar *m.*
Ancient	Qadīm
Anger	<u>Gh</u>ussa *m.*
Angry *adj.*	<u>Kh</u>afā
Ankle	Ta<u>kh</u>na

Annoy	Tañg karnā
Annoyed *adj.*	Nārāz
Annual	Sālāna
Answer	Jawāb
Ant	Chīūñṭī *f.*
Ant (white)	Dīmak *f.*
Anonymous	Gumnām.
Anxiety	Fikr *f.*
Any	Koī *adj.*
Apart	Alag.
Appear	Naẓar ānā.
Appearance	Sūrat.
Application	Ārzī *f.*
Appoint	Muqar-rar karnā *v. tr.*
Apprehend, to	Giriftār karnā
Approval	Manzūrī *f.*
Approve	Manzūr karna
Approximately	Andāzan
Area	Raqba; Ilāqa *m.*
Argue	Hujjat *k. v. tr.*
Arm	Bāzū
Armed *adj.*	Hathyār band
Armpit	Baghal *f.*
Arms	Hathyār
Army	Fauj *f.*
Arrange, to	Band-o-bast *k.*
Arrangement	Band-o-bast
Arrears	Bāqī *f.*
Arrest	Giriftār *k*
Arrest, to be under	Hawālāt mēñ Honā
Arrive	Pahuñchnā
Arsenal	Aslah khāna
Art	Hunar *m.*
Artful	Chālbāz
Artillery	Top khāna *m.*
Ascend	Chaṙhnā
Ascent	Chaṙhāī *f.*
Ascertain	Tahqīq *k.*
Ashamed *adj.*	Sharminda
Ashes	Rākh
Ask	Pūchhnā
Ask for	Māñgnā
Ass	Gadhā
Assist	(ko) madad dēnā
Assist	(ki) Madad karnā
Assure	(ko) Yaqīn dilānā
Attach	Lagānā
Attack	(par) Hamla *k.*
Attempt	Koshish *k.*
Auction	Nīlām *m.*
Authority	Ikhtīār

Avarice	Lālach *m.*
Avaricious *adj.*	Lālchi
Average	Ausat *f.*
Awkward	Anāřī
Axe	Kulhāřī
Axle	Dhura

B

Back	Pīţh *f.*
Back *adv.*	Wāpas
Backwards *adv.*	Pīchhē
Bag	Thailī *f.*
Baggage	Asbāb *m.*
Bail	Zamānat *f.*
Bald	Ganjā
Bamboo	Bāňs *m.*
Banana	Kēlā *m.*
Bandage	Paţţī *f.*
Bank; shore	Kināra *m.*
Banker	Sarrāf *m.*
Bannor	Jhandā *m.*
Barber	Nāī, haj-jām *m.*
Bare (naked)	Naňgā
Bargain	Saudā *m.*
Bark of a tree	Chhāl *f.*
Bark, to	Bhauňknā
Barley	Jau *m.*
Barrel (gun)	Nālī *f.*
Base (mean)	Kamīna
Basket	Ţokra *m.* or Ţokri *f.*
Bath	<u>Gh</u>usl *m.*
Bathe	Nahāňā
Battle	Lařāī *f.*
Bayonet	Saňgīn *f.*
Be, to	Honā
Beak	Choňch *f.*
Bear *v. tr.*	Uţhānā
Bear	Bhālū; rīchh *m.*
Beard	Dāřhī *f.*
Beast	Jānwar *m.*
Beat, to	Mārnā
Beautiful	Khūbsūrat
Beauty	Khūbsūrtī *f.*
Because	Kioňkeh *c.*
Beckon *v. tr.*	Ishāra *k.*
Become, to	Ho jānā
Bed	Palaňg *m.*
Bedding	Bistar *m.*
Beef	Gāč kā gosht *m.*
Before	Sē pahlē or kē sāmnē
Beggar	Faqīr *m.*

Begin	Shurū *k.*	Blind	Andhā
Behaviour	Chāl chalan	Blood	Khūn; lahū *m.*
Behind	Kē pīchhē	Blue	Nīlā
Believe, to	Yaqīn *k.*	Blunt	Kund
Bell	Ghanṭi	Board	Takhta *m.*
Belly	Pēṭ *m.*	Boast *v. tr.*	Shēkhī mārnā
Belt	Peṭī *f.*	Boat	Kishtī *f.*
Bend	Jhuknā; moṛnā	Body	Badan, Jism *m.*
Benefit	Fāeda *m.*	Body (dead)	Lāsh *f.*
Besides	Kē alāwa	Boil	Phoṛā *m.*
Besiege	Ghērnā	Boil *v. int.*	Khaulnā
Bet	Shart *f.*	Boil *v. tr.*	Khaulānā
Better	Behtar	Bold	Dilēr
Between	Kē darmīān	Bone	Haḍḍī *f.*
Beyond	Kē parē; bāhar	Booty	Lūṭ kā māl
Bier	Janāza *m.*	Border	Kīnāra
Bill (account)	Hisāb *m.*	Born (to be)	Paidā honā
Bird	Parinda	Borrow	Qarz lēnā
Bitch	Kutīā *f.*	Bosom	Sīnā *m.*
Bite	Kāṭnā	Both	Donoṅ
Bitter	Kaṛwā	Bough	Shākh
Blacksmith	Lūhār *m.*	Boundless	Bē-had
Blank (paper)	Sādā	Boundary	Had *f.*
Blanket	Kambal *m.*	Bouquet	Guldasta *m.*
Bless	(ko) Du'ā dēnā	Box	Sandūq
		Boy	Laṛkā
Blessing	Du'ā *f.*	Boyhood	Laṛakpan

Brain	Bhēja *m.*
Bran	Chokar
Branch	Shākh
Brass	Pītal
Brave	Bahādur
Bravery	Bahādurī
Bread	Roṭī *f.*
Break	Tořnā
Breakfast	Nāshta; hāzrī
Breast	Chhātī
Breath	Dam; sāňs
Bribe	Rishwat
Brick	Īnṭ *f.*
Bridge	Pul *m.*
Bright	Raushan
Bring	Lānā
Bring up	Pālnā
Broken	Tūṭā hūā
Broom	Jhāřū *f.*
Brother	Bhāī

Buck	Hiran *m.*
Bucket	Bālṭī *f.*
Buffalo	Bhaiňs *f.*
Build	Banānā
Bullet	Golī *f.*
Bullock	Bail *m.*
Bunch	Guch-chhā
Bundle	Gaṭhřī *f.*
Burn *v. tr.*	Jalānā
Burn *v. Int.*	Jalnā
Burden	Bojh
Burst	Phaṭnā
Bury	Dabānā
Bush	Jhāřī *f.*
Business	Kām; kār-o-bār *m.*
But	Lēkin
Butt	Kunda *m.*
Butcher	Qasāī
Buy	Kharīdnā

C

Cage	Pinjra *m.*
Calamity	Āfat *f.*
Calculate	Hisāb lagānā *m.*
Calculation	Hisāb
Call, to	Būlānā

Camel	Ūňṭ *m.*
Camp	Pařāo
Campaign	Lařāī *f.* lām *m.*
Camphor	Kāfūr. *m.*
Canal	Nahr *f.*

Candle	Mom battī *f.*
Cane	Bēṅt (or) Bēd
Cannon	Top *f.*
Cantonment	Chhāonī *f.*
Cap	Ṭopī
Capital (town)	Dārul k͟hilāfā
Capture	Pakaṛnā
Caravan	Qāfla *m.*
Care	Fikr; parwāh
Care, to take	K͟habardār honā
Carefully	Hūshyārī sē
Careless	Bē parwāh
Carpenter	Baṛhaī *m.*
Carriage	Gāṛī *f.*
Carry	Lējānā
Cartridge	Kārtūs *m.*
Case (law)	Muqad-dama.
Case (condition)	Hāl
Cash	Naqd *m.*
Caste	Zāt *f.*
Casualty	Nuqsān(Murdē aur Zak͟hmī)
Cat	Bil-lī
Catch	Pakaṛnā
Cause	Sabab *m.*
Cavalry	Risāla
Cave	G͟hār

Cease	Mauqūf *k.*
Cease fire.	To gola bārī band *k.*
Ceiling	Chhat *f.*
Centre	Bīch or Markaz *m.*
Century	Sadī *f.*
Ceremony	Rasm *f.*
Certainly	Zarūr, Bēshak.
Chain	Zanjīr
Chair	Kursī
Chance	Ittefāq
Change, to	Badalnā
Charcoal	Koelā.
Cheap	Sastā
Cheat, to	Thagnā
Cheese	Panīr *m.*
Chew	Chabānā.
Child	Bach-cha *m.*
Chin	Ṭhoṛī *f.*
Cholera	Haiza *m.*
Choose	Pasand *k.*
Church	Girjā *m.*
Circle	Ghērā *m.*
City	Shahr *m.*
Claim	Dāwā *m.*
Class	Darja

Clean, clear	Sāf
Clever	Hūshyār
Cleverly	Hūshyārī sē
Climb	Chaṙhnā
Clip, to	Kātnā
Clock	Ghanṭa *m.*
Cloth	Kapṙā *m.*
Cold, cool	Ṭhanḍā
Collect	Jama karnā
Commence	Shurū *k.*
Common	Ām, m'āmūlī
Commonly	Amūman
Complain, to	Shikāyat *k.*
Complete	Pūrā
Compound	Ehāta *m.*
Comrade	Sāthī *m.*
Conceal	Chhupānā
Condition	Hālat
Confidently	Itmīnān sē
Consent	Marzī *f.*
Consider	Sochnā
Contagious	Phailnē wālā
Continually	Barābar; musalsal
Contract	Ṭhēka *m.*
Contractor	Ṭhēkēdār
Copy *v. tr.*	Naql *k.*
Cord	Ḍorī *f.*
Corner	Kona *m.*
Correct	Thīk
Count	Ginnā
Country	Mulk *m.*
Country (Rural)	Ḍēhāt
Cover *v. tr.*	Ḍhaknā or Ḍhānknā
Covetous	Lālchī
Cow	Gāē *f.*
Coward	Buzdil; ḍarpok
Cowherd	Goālā; Charwāhā
Cream	Malāī *f.*
Crew	Jahāzī
Crime	Jurm *m.*
Crooked	Ṭeṙhā *adj.*
Crop	Fasl *f.*
Cross	Kē pār jānā
Cross-road	Chaurāha *m.*
Crow	Kawwā *m.*
Crowd	Hujūm
Crown	Tāj *m.*
Cruel	Zālim
Cruelty	Zulm
Cry v. Int.	Ronā, chil-lānā
Culprit	Mujrim *m.*
Cultivation	Khētī *f.*

Cultivator	Kīsān
Cup	Pīāla *m.*
Cunning	Chālāk
Cure *v. tr.*	Ilāj *k.*
Curtain	Parda *m.*
Curve	Mor *m.*
Cushion	Gaddī *f.*
Custom	Dastūr
Customs	Mahsūl *m.*
Customer	Gāhak *m.*
Cut *v. tr.*	Kāṭnā

D

Dacoit	D̄ākū
Daily	Roz marra
Damage	Nuqsān *m.*
Damage *v. tr.*	Nuqsān *k.*
Damp	Namdār
Dance	Nāch *m.*
Dance *v. tr.*	Nāchnā
Danger	D̄ar, k͟hatra *m.*
Dangerous *adj.*	K͟haufnāk
Dark	Andhērā
Date	Tārīk͟h *f.*
Date (fruit)	Khajūr *m.*
Daughter	Bēṭī
Dawn adv.	Din niklē
Day	Din or roz *m.*
Day by day	Roz roz
Dead of night	Ādhi rāt
Deaf *adj.*	Bahrā
Dealing	Lēn dēn *m.*
Dear (expensive)	Maňhgā
Dear (Beloved)	Pīārā
Death	Maut
Debt	Qarz
Debtor	Qarzdār
Deceitful *adj.*	Farēbī
Deceived, to be	Dhoka khānā
Decide *v. tr.*	Faisla *k.*
Decorate *v. tr.*	Sajānā
Deduct *v. tr.*	Kāṭnā
Deep	Gahrā
Deface *v. tr.*	K͟harāb *k.*
Defeat	Shikast *f.*
Defeat *v. tr.*	Shikast *d.*
Defeated, to be	Shikast khānā
Defect	'Aīb *m.*
Defective	'Aībdār
Defence	Bachāo *m.*
Defend	Bachānā

Deficient	Kam
Defile *v. tr.*	Ganda *k.*
Delay *v. tr.*	Dēr *k.*
Delicate	Nāzuk
Delight	<u>Kh</u>ūshī
Delicious	Mazēdār
Demand *v. tr.*	Māṅgnā
Demolish *v. tr.*	Ujāṛnā
Denial	Inkār *m.*
Deny *v. tr.*	(sē) Inkār *k.*
Depart *v. Int.*	Chalnā
Departure	Rawāṅgī *f.*
Department	Mahakma *m.*
Descend *v. Int.*	Utārnā
Describe *v. tr.*	Bayān *k.*
Desert	Sahrā
Desert, to	Bhāg jānā
Deserter	Bhāgoṛā *m.*
Destiny	Qismat *f.*
Destroy *v. tr.*	Barbād *k.*
Devil	Shaitān *m.*
Dew	Os *f.*
Diamond	Hīrā *m.*
Die	Marnā
Difference	Farq *m.*
Different	Mu<u>kh</u>talif
Difficult *adj.*	Mushkil
Diffculty	Mushkil
Dig *v. tr.*	Khodnā

Dirty	Mailā
Disappear *v. Int.*	<u>Gh</u>āib *h.*
Disease	Bīmārī *f.*
Disgrace *v. tr.*	Ruswā karnā
Dishonest	Bē-īmān
Dismiss	Bar<u>kh</u>āst *k.*
Dismissed, to be	Chhuṭnā
Dismount	Utārnā
Disperse	Tit-tar bit-tar *k.*
Displease *v. Int.*	Nā<u>kh</u>ūsh *k.*
Disposition	Mizāj *m.*
Distance	Fāsla *m.*
Distinctly	Sāf sāf.
Distribute *v. tr.*	Bāṅṭnā
District	Zila' *m.*
Ditch	<u>Kh</u>āī; <u>kh</u>andaq
Divide *v. tr.*	Bāṅṭnā
Donkey	Gadhā.
Double *adj.*	Dugnā
Doubt	Shak *m.*
Drain	Nālī.
Drop	Qatra; būnd
Drown *v. tr.*	Dūbnā
Duck	Bat-ta<u>kh</u>
Dung (horse)	Līd *f.*
Dung (cow)	Gobar *m.*
Dust	<u>Kh</u>āk *f.*
Duty	Farz *m.* Naukrī *f.*

E

Each	Har ēk
Ear	Kān
Early	Sawērē
Early in the morning	Subah sawērē
Earn *v. tr.*	Kamānā
Earth (ground)	Zamīn *f.*
Earth (world)	Dunyā *f.*
Earthquake	Bhauṅchāl *m.*
Ease	Ārām
East	Mashriq *f.*
Education	Tālīm
Effects	Asbāb; māl
Effort	Koshish *f.*
Electric pole	Bijlī kā khambā
Elephant	Hāthī
Emperor	Shahanshāh
Empire	Saltanat
Employed, to be	Naukar honā
Employment	Naukrī *f.*
Empty *adj.*	Khālī
Encampment	Paṙāo *m.*
Encamp *v. tr.*	Ḍērē ḍālnā
Enclosure	Baṙā ehāta
Encourage	Himmat dilānā
End of a rope	Rassi ka Sirā *m.*
Endless *adj.*	Bēhad
Enemy	Dushman *m.*
Engagement (battle)	Laṙāī
Engagement (business)	Masrūfīat
Enlist *v. tr.*	Bhartī *k.*
Enmity	Dushmanī
Enough	Kāfī
Enquiry	Tahqīqāt
Enter	Dākhil *h.*
Entirely	Bilkul
Entrench	Morcha banān
Envelope	Lifāfa *m.*
Equal *adj.*	Barābar
Erase *v. tr.*	Miṭānā
Erect *v. tr.*	Khaṙā *k.*
Escape	Bachnā
Especially	Khāskar
Etcetera	Waghaira
Even	Bhī
Evening	Shām
Every	Har
Ever	Kabhī
Evidence	Gawāhī
Evident *adj.*	Zāhir
Evil *adj.*	Burā
Examination	Imtihān *m.*
Examiner	Mumtahin

Example	Misāl
Exceedingly	Nihāyat
Except	Kē siwā
Exercise (Physical)	Warzish *f.*
Exercise (practice)	Mashq *f.*
Excess	Ziādtī
Excuse	Uzr *m.*
Excuse to,	Muāf *k.*
Executioner	Jal-lād *m.*
Exertion	Mehnat *f.*
Expenditure	Kharch *m.*
Expensive *adj.*	Mehn̆gā
Explain *v. tr.*	Samjhānā
Explanation	Bayān *m.* Jawāb *m.*
Extinguish *v. tr.*	Bujhānā
Eye	Ān̆kh *f.*

F

Face	Mun̆h; chehra *m.*
Fact	Asl bāt *f.*
Fair (show)	Mēla
Fair *adj.*	Khāsa
Faithful	Wafādār
Falsehood	Jhūṭ
Family	Kunba *m.*
Famous	Mash-hūr
Fare	Kirāya *m.*
Farrier	Nāl band *m.*
Fat *adj.*	Moṭā
Fate	Qismat *f.*
Fatigue	Thakān
Fault	Qasūr *m.*
Favour	Mehrbānī
Fear	Ḍar *m.*
Fear *v. Int.*	Ḍarnā
Feed *v. tr.*	Khilānā
Felt	Namda *m.*
Female	Māda *f.*
Fence	Bāṛ *f.*
Fever	Bukhār *m.*
Few	Chand
Field (cultivated)	Khēt *m.*
Field (of battle)	Maidān *m.*
Field glasses	Dūrbīn
Fight	Laṛāī *f.*
Fight, to	Laṛnā
Fill *v. tr.*	Bharnā
Filth	Kūṛā
Find *v. tr.*	Pānā
Fine (money)	Jurmānā *m.*
Fine *v. tr.* (par)	Jurmānā *k.*

Fine *adj.*	Umda
Finger	Uṅglī
Finish *v. tr.*	Khatm *k.*
Finish *v. Int.*	Khatm *h.*
Fire	Āg *f.*
First	Pahlā
Flag (big)	Jhanḍā *m.*
Flag (small)	Jhanḍī *f.*
Floor	Farsh *m.*
Flow	Bahnā
Flower	Phūl *m.*
Fly, to	Uṙnā
Foolishness	Bēwaqūfī
Foot of hill	Pahāṙ kā dāman
Forbid *v. Int.*	Mana karnā.
Forest	Jaṅgal.
Forward	Āgē.
Forget *v. Int.*	Bhūlnā
Friday	Jum'a
Friend	Dost.
Front	Sāmnē.

G

Game	Shikār *m.*
Game (play)	Khēl
Garden	Bāgh
Gate	Phāṭak
Gather *v. tr.*	Jama *k.*
Gather *v. Int.*	Jama *h.*
Generally	Aksar
Gently	Āhista sē
Girth	Jisāmat *f.*
Glad *adj.*	Khūsh
Glove	Dastāna *m.*
Goat	Bakrā *m.*
God	Khudā *m.*
Gold	Sonā *m.*
Goodness	Bhalāī,nēkī *f.*
Gonorrhoea	Sozāk *m.*
Goods	Māl *m.*
Govern *v. tr.*	Hukūmat *k.*
Government	Sarkār; *f.* hukūmat *f.*
Government *adj.*	Sarkāri.
Gradually *adj.*	Rafta rafta
Grain	Dāna *m.*
Grape	Aṅgūr *m.*
Grass	Ghāṅs
Gratis	Muft
Gratuity	In'ām *f.*
Grave	Qabr *f.*
Graze	Charnā
Green *adj.*	Harā

Grief	Ranj *m.*
Groom *v. tr.*	Mālish *k.*
Ground	Zamīn *f.*
Groundless *adj.*	Bē bunyād
Grow	Ugnā
Guardian	Muhāfiz
Guest	Mehmān *m.*
Guess *v. tr.*	Qayās *k.*
Guide	Rehnumā *m.*
Guide *v. tr.*	Rāsta batānā
Gun (shot)	Bandūq
Gun (canon)	Top *f.*
Gun-powder	Bārūd

H

Habit	Ādat *f.*
Hair	Bāl
Half *adj.*	Ādhā.
Halt	Muqām *m.*
Handkerchief	Rūmāl *m.*
Handle	Dasta *m.*
Hang (suspend) *v. tr.*	Laṭkānā
Hang (execute) *v. tr.*	(ko) Phāṅsī *d.*
Happen *v. tr.*	Wāqē *h.*
Happiness	Khūshī *f.*
Hard	Sakht
Hare	Khargosh *m.*
Harm	Nuqsān
Harness	Sāz *m.*
Haste	Jaldī *f.*
Hasten	Jaldī *k.*
Hate *v. tr.*	(sē) Nafrat *k.*
Hatred	Nafrat *f.*
Haughty *adj.*	Maghrūr
Haversack	Jholā *m.*
Head	Sir
Health	Sehat *f.*
Healthy	Tandurust
Heap	Dhēr *m.*
Hear, to	Sunnā
Heart	Dil *m.*
Heat	Garmī *f.*
Heaven	Bahisht *f.*
Heavy *adj.*	Bhārī
Hedge	Bāṛ *f.*
Heel	Ēṛī *f.*
Height	Uṅchāī *f.*
Hell	Jahannam *m.*
Help *v. tr.*	(ko) Madad *d.*
Helpless *adj.*	Bēchārah

Hen	Murghī
Herd	Galla *m.*
Hesitation	Jhi-jhak
Hide *v. tr.*	Chhupānā
Hill (single)	Pahāřī *f.*
Hills (Group)	Pahāř *m.*
Hinder *v. tr.*	Roknā
Hire	Kirāya *m.*
History	Tārikh
Hit	Mārnā
Hold *v. tr.*	Pakařnā
Hole (in earth)	Gařhā *m.*
Hole	Chhēd, sūrākh *m.*
Holiday	Chhuṭṭī *f.*
Home (native place)	Watan *m.*
Honesty	Īmāndārī
Honour	Izzat
Hoof	Sum *m.*
Hope	Ummīd
Host	Mēzbān
However	Magar
Human being	Insān *m.*
Hunger	Bhūk *f.*
Hungry *adj.*	Bhūkā
Hunt *v. tr.*	Shikār *k.*
Hurt	Choṭ *f.*
Hurt *v. Int.*	Choṭ lagnā
Hut	Jhoňpřī *f.*

I

Ice	Barf *f.*
Idea	Khīāl *m.*
Idle *adj.*	Sust
Ignorant	Jāhil, nādān
Immediately *adj.*	Fauran
Impatient *adj.*	Bēsabr
Impertinence	Gustākhī *f.*
Impertinent *adj.*	Gustākh
Important *adj.*	Zarūrī
Impossible *adj.*	Nā mumkin
Imprison *v. tr.*	Qaid *k.*
In future *adv.*	Āinda
In charge	Zimmē-wār
Include *v. tr.*	Shāmil *k.*
Income	Āmdanī *f.*
Inconvenience	Taklīf *f.*
Increase *v. tr.*	Bařhānā
Indeed	Bēshak
Infantry	Paidal, palṭan *f.*
Inform *v. tr.*	Khabar dēnā
Information	Khabar

In front	kē sāmnē (or) Āgē wālā
Inhabitant	Bāshinda *m.*
Injure *v. tr.*	Nuqsān *k.*
Injustice	Bē-insāfī *f.*
Ink	Sīāhī *f.*
Inkpot	Dawāt
Inn	Sarāē *f.*
Innocent *adj.*	Bēgunāh
Insect	Kīřā *m.*
Insensible *adj.*	Bē-hosh
Insist *v. tr.*	Zid karnā
Insolent *adj.*	Gustākh
Inspect *v. tr.*	Mulāhiza *k.*
Inspection	Mulāhiza *m.*
Instalment	Qist *f.*
Instead of	Kē badlē
Insufficient	Nā kāfī
Insult *v. tr.*	Bē-izzatī *k.*
Intelligent *adj.*	Aqlmand
Intend *v. tr.*	Irāda *k.*
Intention	Irāda *m.*
Intentional *adj.*	Jān būjh kar
Interest (of money)	Sūd *m.*
Interest (in a matter)	Matlab *m.*
Intoxication	Nasha *m.*
Intrenchment	Nālī, khandaq *f.*
Intrigue	Sāzish *f.*
Invade *v. tr.*	Par hamla *k.*
In vain adv.	Bēfāeda
Invasion	Hamla *m.*
Investigation *v. tr.*	Tahqīqāt *k.*
Inward	Andar kī taraf *f.*
Iron	Lohā *m.*
Irregular *adj.*	Bēqāeda
Island	Ṭāpū; Jazīra *m.*
Issue (an order)	Jārī *k.*

J

Jackal	Gīdař *m.*
Jaw	Jabřā *m.*
Jealous *adj.*	Hāsid
Jerk *v. tr.*	Jhaṭkā mārnā
Jester	Maskharā *m.*
Jewel	Zēwar *m.*
Joint n.	Joř
Joke *v. tr.*	Mazāq *k.*
Journey	Safar *m.*
Joy	Khūshi *f*
Jump *v. tr.*	Kūdnā
Justice	Insāf *m.*

K

Keen	Shauqīn	Kindness	Mehrbānī *f.*
Keep	Rakhnā	Kindly	Mehrbānī sē
Kettle	Kētlī *f.*	King	Bādshāh
Key	Chābī *f.*	Kingdom	Bādshāhat
Kick (man)	Thokar mārnā	Kitchen	Bawarchī-khāna *m.*
Kick (of horse) *v. tr.*	Lāt mārnā	Kite (bird)	Chīl *f.*
Kill	Mār d̄ālnā	Knee	Ghuṭna *m.*
Killed	Mār jānā	Know	Jānnā
Kind (sort)	Qism *f.*	Knowingly *adj.*	Jān būjh kar
Kind *adj.*	Mehrbān	Knowledge	Ilm *m.*

L

Labour	Mehnat *f.*	Lend	Qarz dēnā
Ladder	Sīṙhī *f.*	Less	Kam
Lake	Jhīl *f.*	Lesson	Sabaq
Lame *adj.*	Laṅgṙā	Letter	Chiṭ-ṭhī *f.*
Land	Zamīn		Khat *m.*
Language	Zabān *f.*	Lick *v. tr.*	Chāṭnā
Law	Qānūn	Lie (animate)	Lēṭnā
Leaf	Patta *m.*	(inanimate)	Paṙnā
Learn *v. tr.*	Sikhnā	Life	Jān *f.*
Leather	Chamṙā *m.*	Light	Roshnī *f.*
Leave	Chhuṭ-ṭī *f.*	Light *adj.*	Halkā
Leave *v. tr.*	Chhoṙnā	Light *v. tr.*	Jalānā
Left	Bāyāṅ	Like *v. tr.*	Pasand karnā
Leg	Tāṅg *f.*	Like *adv.*	Kī tarach
Leisure	Fursat *f.*	Likewise	Is hī taran

Limit	Had *f.*	Look	Dēkhnā
List	Fehrist	Look for	Talāsh *k.*
To live (dwell) *v. int.*	Rahnā	Loose *adj.*	Ḍhīlā
To live (exist) *v. int.*	Jīnā	Lose *v. tr.*	Khonā
Load	Bojh *m.*	Lose (a bet) *v. tr.*	Hārnā
Load *v. tr.*	Lādnā	Loss	Nuqsān
Lock, to	Tālā lagānā	Luck	Qismat *f.*

M

Mad *adj.*	Pāgal	Message	Paighām *m.*
Mail train	Ḍāk gāṛī *f.*	Method	Tarīqa *m.*
Mango tree	Ām kā darakht	Middle	Bīch; wast
Manner	Tarīqa *m.*	Mile	Mīl *f.*
March *v. tr.*	Kūch karnā	Military	Fauj *f.*
Mark	Nishān *m.*	Mind	Dil *m.*
Marriage	Shādī *f.*	Mischief	Sharārat *f.*
Marry *v. tr.*	Sē shādī *k.*	Miserly *adj.*	Kanjūs *f.*
Master (owner)	Mālik	Misfortune	Musībat *f.*
Matter	M'uāmlā *m*	Missing	Kam, ghāib
Measure *v. tr.*	Nāpnā	Mistake	Ghalati *f.*
Meat	Gosht *m.*	Mix *v. tr.*	Milānā
Medal	Tamgha *m.*	Money (ready)	Naqd *m.*
Meddle	Ḍākhl dēnā	Monkey	Bandar *m.*
Medical	Ḍākṭar kā or Tib-bī	Month	Mahīna
		Moon	Chānd *m.*
Medicine	Dawā *f.*	Mount *v. tr.*	Chaṛhnā
Mend *v. tr.*	Marammat *k.*	Mountain	Pahāṛ
Merchant	Saudāgar or Tājir	Mouth	Muṅh *m.*
		Mud	Kīchar

Muddy *adj.*	Gadlā
Mule	Khach-char *m.*
Murder	Qatl *k.*
Mosquito	Mach-chhar *m.*
Mount, to	Charhnā
Mutiny	Ghadar *m.*

N

Nail	Kīl *f.*
Nail (of finger)	Nākhun *m.*
Naked *adj.*	Naňgā
Narrow *adj.*	Taňg
Nation	Qaum *f.*
Native *adj.*	Dēsī
Navy	Behrī Beřā *m.*
Necessary *adj.*	Zarūrī *f.*
Necessity	Zarūrat
Neck	Gardan *f.*
Neglect *v. tr.*	Ghaflat *k.*
Neighbour	Pařausī *m.*
Neighbourhood	Pařaus *m.*
Net	Jāl *m.*
News	Khabar *f.*
Noble *adj.*	Sharīf
Noise	Shor *m.*
Nonsense	Wāhīāt *f.*
Noon	Do pahar
North	Shumāl *m.*
Nose	Nāk *f.*
Nowadays	Āj kal
Now and then	Kabhī kabhī
Nuisance	Wabāl *m.*
Number	Gintī, *f.* tedād *f.*
Numerous *adj.*	Bēshumār

O

Oath (to take an)	Qasm khānā
Obey *v. Int.* (hukm)	Mānnā
Object	Matlab *m.*
Object *v. tr.*	Etrāz *k.*
Oblique	Teřhā; Tirchhā
Obtain	Hāsil *k.*
Occasion	Mauqa *m.*
Occupation	Pēsha *m.*
Offend, to *v. tr.*	Nārāz *k.*
Official *adj.*	Sarkārī
Often *adv.*	Āksar
Old age	Buřhāpā
Once	Ēk dafa
Only	Sirf
Open, to	Kholnā
Openly *adv.*	Zāhir mēň
Ordinary	Māmūlī
Opinion	Rāē *f.*
Opportunity	Mauqa *m.*
Opposite	Sāmnē

Oppress *v. tr.*	Satānā
Oral	Zabānī
Order (method)	Tartīb
(command)	hukm
Orderly	Ardalī *m.*
Original	Asl
Ornament	Zēwar *m*
Otherwise	Warna
Outward	Bāhar kī taraf
Owner	Mālik *m.*
Ox	Bail *m.*

P

Pace	Qadam *m.*
Pack *v. tr.*	Bāndhnā
Page	Safha *m.*
Pain	Dard
Pains, to take	Mehnat karnā
Paint	Rang *m.*
Pair Pole *Adj.*	Jořā *m.*
Palm tree	Khajūr kā darakht
Panic	Sakht ghabrāhaṭ
Parade	Qawāid, parēḍ
Pardon, to *v. tr.*	Mu'āf *k.*
Parents	Māñ bap
Part	Hissa *m.*
Particular *adj.*	Khās kar
Particularly *adj.*	Khās kar
Partridge	Tītar *m.*
Pass *v. Int.*	Guzarnā
Pass *v. tr.*	Guzarnā
Passage	Rāsta *m.*
Passenger	Musāfir *m.*
Patience	Sabr *m.*
Pay	Tankhwāh; Talab *f.*
Peace	Sulah *f.*
Peacock	Mor *m.*
People (plural)	Log
Perfectly	Bilkul
Permission	Ijāzat
Person	Shakhs *m.*
Petition	Arzī
Picture	Taswīr *f.*
Piece	Ṭukřā *m.*
Pigeon	Kabūtar *m.*
Pillow	Takya *m.*
Pipal tree	Pīpal kā darakht
Pit	Gařhā *m.*
Place	Jagah *f.*
Play *v. tr.*	Khēlnā
Pleader	Vakīl
Please, to	Khūsh *k.*
Pleasure *v. tr.*	Khūshī
Plunder *v. tr.*	Lūtnā
Pocket	Jēb
Poet	Shair
Poem	Nazm
Point out *v. tr.*	Batlānā

Point at	Ishāra *k.*
Port	Bandargāh
Poplar tree	Chunār kā darakht
Potato	Ālū *m.*
Pour *v. tr.*	Ḍālnā
Powder (Gun)	Bārūd *f.*
Power	Tāqat *f.*
Praise	Tārīf
Preparation	Taiyārī
Prepare, to	Taiyār *k.*
Present	Hāzīr
Pretend *v. tr.*	Bahāna *k.*
Prevent *v. tr.*	Roknā
Previously	Pahlē
Price	Qīmat *f.*
Profit	Fāeda; nafa
Prohibit *v. tr.*	Mana *k.*
Promise	W'āda *m.*
Promptly	Phurtī se
Property	Māl *m.*
Proof	Sabūt *m.*
Proud *adj.*	Maghrūr
Publish *v. tr.*	Shā'i *k.*
Pull *v. tr.*	Khēňchnā
Punish *v.tr.*	Sazā *d.*
Purpose	Matlab *m.*
Push	Dhakkā *d.*

Q

Quail	Baṭēr
Quarrel	Jhagřā *m.*
Quarrel *v. Int.*	Jhagařnā
Queen	Malka *f.*
Question	Sawāl *m.*
Queer *adj.*	Ājīb
Question *v. tr.*	Sawāl *k.*
Quickly	Jaldī se
Quietly	Chupkē se
Quite *adv.*	Bilkul

R

Race (Horse)	Ghuřdauř
Race (tribe)	Qaum *f.*
Rain *f.'*	barish, Mēňh *m.*
Rain *v. Int.*	Mēňh barasnā
Rainy season	Barsāt *f.*
Raise	Uṭhānā
Random (at)	Aṭkal pachchū
Range of hills	Pahāřioň kā Silsila
Range, striking distance	Mār
Rank	Darja, ohda *m.*
Rat	Chūhā
Rate	Nirkh; bhāo *m*
Raw *adj.*	Kachchā
Real	Aslī
Reasonable	Munāsib
Rebel	Bāghī *m.*

Rebel *v. tr.*	Baghāwat
Receipt	Rasīd
Recently	Hāl hī mēn̆
Recognize *v. tr.*	Pahchānnā
Recommend *v. tr.*	Sifārish *k.*
Recruit	Ran̆grūṭ
Refuse *v. tr.*	(se) Inkār *k.*
Regiment	Palṭan *f.*
Regret v. Int.	Pachhtānā
Reins	Bāg *f.*
Relation	Rishta *m.*
Relative	Rishtedār *m.*
Release *v. tr.*	Chhoṙnā
Religion	Mazhab *m.*
Remember *v. tr.*	Yād *k.*
Remind *v. tr.*(ko)	Yād dilānā
Rent	Kirāya
Repairs	Marammat *f.*
Repair *v. tr.*	Kī Marammat *k.*
Repeatedly *adv.*	Bār bār
Repent *v. tr.*	(sē) Pachhtānā
Report *v. tr.*	K͟habar dēnā
Request *v. tr.*	Dark͟hwāst *k.*
Resign *v. tr.*	Isṭīfa dēnā
Resignation	Isṭīfa *m.*
Resist *v. tr.*	Roknā
Responsible *adj.*	Zimmēwār
Rest	Ārām *m.*
Rest *v. tr.*	Ārām *k.*
Restless *adj.*	Bē chain
Result	Natīja *m.*
Revenge	Badla *m.*
Revenge	(se) Badla lēnā
Reward	In 'ām
Reward *v.tr.*	In 'ām *d.*
Rice	Chāwal *m.*
Ride *v. tr.*	Sawār *h.*
Riches	Daulat *f.*
Rifle	Rāifal *f.*
Right (Proper)	Ṭhīk
Right (not left) *adj.*	Dāyān̆ or Dāhnā
Ripe *adj.*	Pakkā
Rise *v. Int.*	Uṭhnā; nikalnā
River	Daryā *m.*
Road Metalled	Saṙak
Roar	Dhāṙ *f.*
Rob *v. tr.*	Lūṭnā
Robber	Ḍākū *m.*
Robbery	Ḍāka
Rock	Chaṭān *f.*
Roof	Chhat *f.*
Root	Jaṙ *f.*
Rope	Rassī *f.*
Rotten *adj.*	Saṙā hūā
Round *adj.*	Gol
Row (a line)	Qatār *f.*
Royal	Shāhī
Rub *v. tr.*	Malnā
Rubbish	Kūṙā *m.*
Ruin *v. tr.*	Barbād *k.*
Rule	Qāeda *m.*
Rush	Jhapaṭnā
Rust	Zang *m.*

S

Saddle	Zīn
Safe *adj.*	Salāmat, mahfūz
Safety	Hifāzat
Salt	Namak *m.*
Salutation	Salām *m.*
Salute *v. tr.*	Ko salām *k.*
Same	Woh hī; ēk hī
Sample	Namūna
Sand	Rēt *f.*
Satisfy *v. tr.*	Mutma 'in k
Satisfactory	Qābil-e-itminān
Save *v. tr.*	Bachānā
Scar	Dāgh *m.*
Scatter *v. tr.*	Bakhernā
Scissors	Qaīṅchī *f.*
Scratch *v. tr.*	Khujānā
Screw	Pēch *m.*
Screw-driver	Pēch kash *m.*
Search *v. tr.*	Talāsh *k.*
Season	Mausam *m.*
Secret	Bhēd, rāz *m.*
Secretly *adv.*	Chupkē sē
Seed	Bīj
Select *v. tr.*	Chhāṅṭnā
Sell	Bēchnā
Send	Bhējnā
Send (for person)	Bulānā
Send (for thing)	Maṅgwānā
Sense	Hosh *m.*

Senseless	Bēhosh
Separate *v. tr.*	Judā *k.*
Separately adv.	Judā judā
Serve *v. tr.*	Naukrī *k.*
Service	Naukrī *f.*
Settle (account)	Chukānā
Several *adj.*	Kai
Severe	Sakht
Sew *v. tr.*	Sinā
Shade (shadow)	Sāyā *m.*
Shake *v. tr.*	Hilānā
Shame	Sharm *f.*
Shameless *adj.*	Bēsharm
Share	Hissa *m.*
Sharpen *v. tr.*	Tēz karnā
Sheet (bed)	Chādar *f.*
Ship	Jahāz *m.*
Shirt	Qamīz
Shoe	Jūtā
Shoe (horse)	Nāl
Shore	Kinārā
Shorts	Jāṅgīā, nēkar *m.*
Shoulder	Kandhā *m.*
Shout	Chil-lānā
Show	Dikhānā
Shut	Band *k.*
Sick	Bīmār
Sickness	Bīmārī *f.*
Side	Taraf *f.*
Side (of person)	Pahlū *m.*

Seize *v. tr.*	Pakaṙnā
Sight; show	Tamāsha
Sign *v. tr.*	Ishāra *k.*
Sign (a paper) *v. tr.* (par)	Dastkhat *k.*
Signature	Dastkhat *m.*
Silence	Khāmoshī *f.*
Silent *adj.*	Chup
Silk	Rēsham
Silver	Chāndī *f.*
Sin	Gunāh *m.*
Sing *v. Int.*	Gānā
Single file	Ēk qatār
Sink	Dūbnā
Sister	Bahen
Sit	Baiṭhnā
Skilful *adj.*	Hūshyār
Skin	Khāl *f.*
Sky	Āsmān *m.*
Slave	Ghulām. *m.*
Sleep	Nīnd *f.*
Sleep, to	Sonā
Sleeve	Āstīn
Slip *v. Int.*	Phisalnā
Slow	Dhīmā; āhista
Smell *v. tr.*	Sūṅghnā
Smoke	Dhūān *m.*
Snake	Sāṅp
Snatch *v. tr.*	Chhīn lēnā
Snipe	Chāha
Sock	Moza *m.*
Soft	Narm
Some	Kuchh

Sometimes	Kabhī Kabhī
Somewhere	Kahīṅ
Sorrow	Afsos
Sort	Qism *f.*
Soup	Shorbā *m.*
South	Junūb
Spare *adj.*	Fāltū
Special	Khās
Speed	Raftār *f.*
Spend *v. tr.*	Kharch *k.*
Spit *v. tr.*	Thūknā
Spoil *v. tr.*	Bigāṙnā; barbād karnā
Spoon	Chamcha *m.*
Spread *v. tr.*	Phailānā
Spread *v. Int.*	Phailnā
Spy	Jāsūs *m.*
Squander *v. tr.*	Barbād *k.*
Stable	Astabal *m.*
Stale *adj.*	Bāsī
Stand *v. Int.*	Khaṙā *h.*
Start	Rawanā hona
Statement	Bayān *m.*
Steal *v. tr.*	Churānā
Step	Qadam
Step out, to	Qadam baṙhānā
Stone	Pat-thar *m.*
Stop	Roknā
Storm	Tūfān
Storm (wind)	Āndhī
Story	Kahānī *f.*
Storey (of house)	Manzil *f.*
Straight *adj.*	Sīdhā
Stranger	Ghair ādmī *m.*

Strap	Tasma *m.*
Stream	Naddī *f.*
Strength	Tāqat *f.*
Strike	Mārnā
Student	Tālib-e-ilm
Submarine	D̄ubaknī kishtī
Success	Kāmyābī
Successful	Kāmyāb *h.*
Such	Aisā
Summer	Garmī *f.*
Sun	Sūraj *m.*
Sun-shine	Dhūp
Suspiciously	Shak kē sāth
Sweets	Mithāī
Sword	Talwār *f.*
Sympathy	Hamdardī *f.*

T

Tail	Dum
Tall	Lambā
Take	Lēnā
Take off	Utārnā
Take out	Nikālnā
Tank	Tālāb *m.*
Tape	Fīta *m.*
Target	Nishāna
Teach *v. tr.*	Sikhānā
Telegram	Tār *m.*
Temper	Mizāj *m.*
Temporary *adj.*	Ā'rzī
Tent	Dēra; tambū
Terrible	Khaufnāk
Theft	Chorī
Therefore	Is wāstē; Is līē
Thick *adj.*	Moṭā
Thigh	Rān; jāňgh *f.*
Thin, lean	Dublā, patlā *m.*
Thing	Chīz *f.*
Think *v. tr.*	Khiāl *k.*
Thirsty	Piāsā
Thorn	Kāňṭā *m.*
Thought	Khiāl
Thousand	Hazār
Threaten *v. tr.*	Dhamkī *d.*
Throat	Galā
Throw *v. tr.*	Phēňknā
Thumb	Aňgūthā *m.*
Thunder	Garaj *f.*
Thus *adv.*	Is tarah
Tiger	Shēr
Tie *v. tr.*	Bāndhnā
Tigress	Shērnī
Tight *adj.*	Taňg
Time	Waqt.
Time (leisure)	Fursat *f.*
Tongue	Zabān *f.*
Tooth	Dāňt *m.*
Top of hill	Pahāř kī choṭī
Torment	Satānā
Touch *v. tr.*	Chhūnā
Tour	Daura *m.*
Towards	Kī taraf
Towel	Taulīa *m.*
Tower	Burj *m.*

Transport	Bār bardārī	Trick	Chāl *f.*
Travel *v. tr.*	Safar	Trouble	Taklīf *f.*
Treasury	Khazāna	Trousers	Patlūn or Paejāma
Traveller	Musāfir	Try *v. tr.*	Koshish *k.*
Treat *v. tr.*	Salūk *k.*	Tunnel	Surañg
Treatment (Medical)	Ilāj	Turn	Ghumānā
Tremble *v. Int.*	Kāñpnā	Tyranny	Zulm *m.*
Trench	Morcha	Tyrant	Zālim
Tribe	Qabīla *m.*		

U

Ugly	Badsūrat	Unreasonable	Bējā
Unaware	Bēkhabar	Unsafe	Khatarnāk
Unconscious	Bēhosh	Unusual	Ghair māmūlī
Understand	Samajhnā	Upper	Ūpar kā
Undoubtedly	Bēshak	Urgent *adj.*	Zarūrī
Unfit *adj.*	Nāqābil	Urine	Pēshāb
Unfortunate	Bad qismatī sē	Use (benefit)	Fāeda
Uniform	Wardī *f.*	Use *v. tr.*	Istemāl *k.*
Union	Anjuman *f.*	Useless	Betāeda
Unintentionally	Nādānista	Usual *adv.*	Māmūlī
Unopposed	Bē rok ṭok	Usually	Amūman
Unpleasant	Nāgawār	Utensil	Bartan *m.*

V

Vacant *adj.*	Khālī	Verification	Tasdīq *f.*
Vaccinate	Tīka lagānā	Vicious	Badzāt
Value	Qīmat	Victory	Fatah, Jīt *f.*
Valuable *adj.*	Qīmtī	Victorious	Fatehmand
Vegetable	Tarkārī	Village	Gāoñ *m.*
Verbal	Zabānī	Vinegar	Sirka *m.*

Virtue	Nēkī *f.*	Vow	Ahd *m.*
Voice	Āwāz *f.*	Vulture	Gidh
Vomit *v. tr.*	Qai *k.*		

W

Waist	Kamar *f.*	Widow	Bēwa
Wall	Dīwār *f.*	Width	Chaur̤āī *f.*
War	Lar̤āī *f.*	Wife	Bīwī
Warn	Tan̆bīh	Wild	Jan̆glī
Wash *v. tr.*	Dhonā	Wilfully	Jān būjh kar
Waste *v. tr.*	Barbād *k.*	Willingly *adj.*	Khūshī sē
Weapon	Hathīār *m.*	Win *v. tr.*	Jītnā
Weather	Mausam *m.*	Wind	Hawā *f.*
Wedding	Shādī *f.*	Winding	Mor̤dār
Weight *v. tr.*	Tolnā	Window	Khir̤kī *f.*
Weight	Wazan *m.*	Wine	Sharāb
Well	Kūān̆ *m.*	Wing	Bāzū *m.*
Well *adj.*	Tandurust	Winter	Jār̤ā *m.*
Well-known *adj.*	Mashhūr	Wipe *v. tr.*	Pon̆chhnā
West	Maghrib	Wire	Tār *m.*
Whatever	Jo kuchh	Wisdom	Aql *f.*
Whenever	Jab kabhī	Wise	Aqlmand
Wherever	Jahān̆ kahīn̆	Without	Kē baghair
Wheel	Pahīya *m.*	Witness	Gawāh *m.*
Whip	Chābuk *m.*	Wolf	Bhēr̤iā *m.*
Whistle *v. tr.*	Sīṭī bajānā	Wonder *v. tr.*	Ta'ajjub *k.*
Whistle *f.*	Sīṭī	Wonderful *adj.*	Ajīb
White	Safēd	Wood	Lakr̤ī *f.*
Whole	Sab; Tamām	Woollen *adj.*	Ūnī
Wick *f.*	Battī	Word	Lafz *m.*
Wicked	Badmāsh	Work	Kām

World	Dunyā *f.*	Wrath	G͟hussa *m.*
Wound	Zak͟hm *m.*	Wrist	Kalāī *f.*
Wounded *adj.*	Zak͟hmī	Write	Likhnā
Wrap *v. tr.*	Lapēṭnā	Wrong *adj.*	G͟halat

Y

Yard	Gaz	Yet	Abhī tak; phir bhī
Year	Sāl	Yoke	Jūā *m.*
Yearly *adv.*	Har sāl	Yoke *v. tr.*	Jotnā
Yellow *adj.*	Pīlā, zard	Young	Jawān
Yesterday	Kal	Youth	Jawānī *f.*

Z

Zeal	Sargarmī *f.*	Zigzag	Pēchdār; Moř toř kar
Zealous *adj.*	Sargarm	Zinc	Jast *m.*

VOCABULARY

(B) URDU—ENGLISH

A

Achānak	Suddenly	'Aqlmand	Wise
Adab *k.*	To respect	Aksar *adv.*	Often
Adālat	Court	Aman	Peace
Ādat *f.*	Habit	Amīr	Rich
Afsar *f.*	Officer	Andar	Inside
Afwāh *f.*	Rumour	Andhā	Blind
Āg *f.*	Fire	Andhērā	Dark
Agar	If	Āňkh *f.*	Eye
Agarche	Although	Āṙ *f.*	Shelter
Āgē	Ahead	Ārām	Ease, rest
Āinda	In future	Arzī *f.*	Application
Aisā	Such	Āsān	Easy
Ajīb	Wondeful	Asbāb	Baggage
Āj kal	Nowadays	Ausat *f.*	Average
Akēlā	Alone	Awwal	First

B

Bābat	Concerning	Bahādur	Brave
Bachcha	Child	Bahādurī *f.*	Bravery
Bachnā *Intr.*	To escape	Bāhar	Out
Bachānā *v. tr.*	To save	Bahen *f.*	Sister
Bā'd	After	Bahnā	To flow
Badalnā	Change	Bail	Bullock
Bādla	Revenge	Baiṭhnā	To sit
Bādshāh	King	Bāqāeda	Regular
Bāgh	Garden	Bāqī	Remainder; Balance
Bāghair	Without		

Bakrā	Goat (he)	Bē khabar	Unaware
Bakrī	Goat (she)	Bhāgnā	To run away
Bāl	Hair	Bhāī	Brother
Balke	But	Bharnā	To fill
Banānā	To make	Bhauṅknā	To bark
Band k.	To shut	Bhējnā	To send
Bandal	Bundle	Bhī	Even, also
Bandar	Monkey	Bhīk f.	Alms
Bāp	Father	Bhūlnā	To forget
Barābar	Equal	Bīch	Middle
Barbād k.	To destroy	Bilkul	Quite
Bārish	Rain	Bīmār	Sick
Bartan	Utensil	Bistar	Bedding
Bāsaṭh	Sixty-two	Bīwī f.	Wife
Bāt	Matter, talk	Botal f.	Bottle
Bāwarchī-khāna	Kitchen	Bukhār	Fever
Bēchnā	To sell		

C

Chabānā	To chew	Chhāonī f.	Cantonment
Chādar f	Sheet	Chhoṛnā	To leave
Chāqū	Knife (Pen)	Chhūnā	To touch
Chālāk	Active; cunning	Chhupānā	To hide
		Chil-lānā	To cry; shout
Chalnā	To walk; to start	Chokar f.	Bran
		Chor	Thief
Chalānā	To make go; to drive	Chup	Silent
		Chupkā	Quietly
Chaṛhnā	To get on	Chūnāṅche	Accordingly
Chauṛā	Wide	Chūnke	Since; because
Chaurāha m.	Cross road		
Chhat f.	Roof	Churānā	To steal

D

Dabānā	To bury; to press
Dāgh	Scar
Dakhl *d.*	To meddle
D̄ākū	Dacoit
D̄ākya	Postman
Dālnā	To pour; to drop
Dām	Price
Dāna	Grain
Dāňt	Tooth
Darakht	Tree
Dard	Pain
Dāřhī *f.*	Beard
Darja *m.*	Grade, rank; class
Darmīān	Between
D̄arpok	Cowardly
Daryā	River
Daryāft *k.*	To find out
Dastkhat	Signature
Dastūr	Custom
Daulat *f.*	Wealth
Daulatmand	Wealthy
Daura	Tour
Dauřnā	To run
Dawā or Dawāī	Medicine
Dawāt *f.*	Inkpot
Dēkhnā	To see
Dēra	Tent
Dhoka	Deceit
Dhonā	To wash
Dhund̄nā	To search
Dhūp *f.*	Sunshine
Dikhānā	To show
Dil	Heart
Din	Day
Dīwār *f.*	wall
Dūbnā	To be drowned
Dūdh	Milk
Dum *f.*	Tail
Dukān *f.*	Shop
Dunyā *f.*	World
Dūrbīn *f.*	Telescope
Dushman	Enemy

E

Ehāta	Enclosure; compound
Ekā ēkī	All of a sudden
Etbār	Trust

F

Farq	Difference
Farsh	Floor
Fāsla	Distance
Fauj	Army
Fauran	At once
Fī	Per
Fikr *f.*	Anxiety, worry
Fursat *f.*	Leisure

G

Gadhā	Donkey
Gāē *f.*	Cow
Ghaflat *f.*	Neglect
Gahrā	Deep
Ghalatī *f.*	Mistake
Gālī *f.*	Abuse
Ghāliban	Probably
Gānā	To sing
Gāoň	Village
Gardan *f.*	Neck
Gařhā	Pit
Gawāh	Witness
Gawāhī *f.*	Evidence
Ghanṭa	Hour, clock
Ghanṭī *f.*	Bell
Ghāňs *f.*	Grass
Ghāt *f.*	Ambush
Ghuřdauř *f.*	Race (horse)
Ghuṭnā	Knee
Ginnā	To count
Girānā	To drop
Gird (pre)	Round
Giriftār *k.*	To arrest
Girjā	Church
Girnā	To fall
Gol *adj.*	Round
Golī *f.*	Bullet
Gosht	Meat
Guch-chhā	Bunch
Gumnām	Anonymous
Gunāh	Sin
Ghusl khāna	Bathroom
Gustākh	Impertinent

H

Hafta	Week; Saturday
Hajāmat *f.*	Shaving
Hāl	Account, state
Hāměň (accusative)	Us
Hamēsha	Always
Hamla	Attack
Haňsnā	To laugh

Har	Every; each
Haṭānā *tr.*	To drive away To remove
Haṭnā (*Int.*)	To get out of the way
Hāth *m.*	Hand
Hathyār *m.*	Weapon, arms
Hawā	Air
Hawāī	Aerial
Hazār	Thousand
Hāzir	Present; muster
Hāzirī	Presence
Hifāzat *f.*	Protection
Hilānā	To shake
Hiran	Buck
Hisāb	Account
Hūshyār	Clever
Hūshyārī sē	Cleverly
Hujūm	Crowd; mob

I

Ijāzat *f.*	Permission
Ilm	Knowledge
Imāndār	Honest
Inām	Reward
Inkār	Refuse
Iṙāda	Intention
Ishāra	Sign
Is līe	Therefore
Itnē mēṅ	Meanwhile
Ittifāqan	By chance
Itwār	Sunday
Izzat *f.*	Honour

J

Jagah *f.*	Place
Jagānā *tr.*	To awaken
Jāgnā *Int.*	To wake oneself
Jahāz	Ship
Jau	Oats
Jalānā *tr.*	To burn; light
Jalnā *Int.*	To burn
Jama *k.*	To collect
Jānnā	To know
Jānwar	Animal
Jāsūs	Spy
Jawāb	Reply
Jawān	Young
Jēb *f.*	Pocket
Jēl *f.*	Jail
Jhanḍā	Flag (large)
Jhanḍī *f.*	Flag (small)
Jhapaṭnā	To rush
Jhāṙī *f.*	Bush
Jhaṭkā	Jerk
Jhūṭ	Falsehood
Jhūṭā	Liar

Jīnā	To live; exist
Jītnā	To win
Jo kuchh	Wahtever
Jurm	Crime; offence
Jurmāna	Fine
Jūtī *f.*	Shoe

K

Kab	When
Kabhī	Ever
Kabhī kabhī	Sometimes
Kabūtar	Pigeon
Kāfī	Enough
Kahāň	Where
Kahīň	Somewhere
Kahnā	To tell, to say
Kaī	Several
Kal	Tomorrow
Kam	Less
Kām	Work
Kām-chor	Shirker
Kamānā	To earn
Kāmyāb	Successful
Kamzor	Weak
Kanjūs	Miserly
Kārtūs	Cartridge
Kāṭnā	To cut; bite
Kaun	Who
Kaunsā	Which
Kawwā	Crow
Keh	That
Kētlī	Kettle
Khabar *f.*	News
Khafā	Angry
Khālī	empty
Khānā	To eat; food
Khāňsī *f.*	Cough
Khāňsnā	To cough
kharāb	Bad
Kharch	Expense
Kharīdnā	To buy
Khat	Letter
Khātir	Mind
Khātir jama rakhna	To be at one's ease
Khāwind	Husband
Khīāl *m.*	Thought
Khazāna	Treasury
Khēnchnā	To pull; draw
Khēt	Field
Khilāf	Against
Khiṙkī *f.*	Window
Khodnā	To dig
Khoj	Track
Khoj nikālnā	To track
Khojī	Tracker
Kholnā	To open
Khūb (*adv.*)	Well
Khūbsūrat	Beautiful
Khuda	God
Khūsh	Happy

Khūshī sē	Happily
Kīā	What
Kināra	Bank, shore
Kīoň	Why
Kīoňke	Because
Kirāya	Rent; fare
Kishtī *f.*	Boat
Kiskā	Whose
Kitāb *f.*	Book
Koela	Charcoal
Koī	Any
Kona	Corner
Koshish *f.*	Try
Kūāň	Well
Kuchh	Some
Kuchh nahīň	Nothing
Kursī	Chair
Kutyā	Bitch

L

Lādnā	To load
Lafz	Word
Lagānā	To put on; apply; affix; attach
Laňgřā	Lame
Lařāī *f.*	Fight
Lāṭhī *f.*	Stick
Lēkin	But
Lēṭnā	To lie down
Lifāfa	Envelope
Likhnā	To write
Log	People
Lūṭnā	To rob

M

Madad *f.*	Help
Maghrūr	Proud
Mahīna	Month
Mahsūl	Tax; duty
Mal	Property
Mālik	Owner
Malnā	To rub
Mālūm *h.*	To be known
Mālūm *k.*	To find out
Māň *f.*	Mother
Māň bāp	Parents
Mana *k.*	To forbid
Mandar *m.*	Temple (Hindu)
Māňgnā	To ask for
Mahňgā	Expensive
Marammat *f.*	Repairs
Marnā	To die
Mārnā	To strike; hit
Mār ďalnā	To kill
Mash-hūr	Well known
Mashīn *f.*	Machine
Masjid *f.*	Mosque

Mazāq	Joke
Mazbūt	Strong
Mazdūr	Labourer
Mazdūrī *f.*	Wages
Mehmān	Guest
Mehnat *f.*	Hard work
Mehrbān *adj.*	Kind
Mehrbānī sē	Kindly
Mēla	Fair
Miţhāī *f.*	Sweets
Mizāj	Temperament
Mol lēnā	To buy
Mor	Peacock
Morcha	Trench
Moza	Sock
Muāfī *f.*	Pardon
Muāfiq *f.*	According to
Mujhē (Accusative)	Me
Mulāheza	Inspection
Mulk	Country
Mulzim	Accused
Mumkin	Possible
Muňh	Mouth
Murghī *f.*	Hen
Musāfir	Traveller
Mushkil *adj.*	Difficult
Musībat *f.*	Misfortune
Muskurānā	To smile

N

Nāch *m.*	Dance
Nahānā	To bathe
Nahr *f.*	Canal
Naql *k.*	To copy.
Naqsha *m.*	Map
Nāl *f.*	Shoe (horse)
Nālband	Shoe smith
Nālī *f.*	Barrel, drain
Namak	Salt
Namak harām	Traitor; disloyal
Namāz *f.*	Prayer, service
Narm	Soft
Nayā	New
Nazdik	Near
Nīchā	Low
Nīchē	Under
Nikalnā	To come out
Nikālnā	To take out; to turn out
Nirkh	Rate
Nishān	Mark; sign

O

Ohda	Rank; grade
Ohdēdār	Official
Ola	Hail
Os *f.*	Dew

P

Pahāṙ	Mountain	Paṙnā	To fall
Pahchānnā	To recognise	Parsoṅ	Day after tomorrow
Pehannā	To put on; to wear	Pasand *k.*	To like
Pahrā	Duty (watch)	Pata	Address; trace
Pahuṅchnā	To reach	Patta	Leaf
Pahuṅchānā	To make reach	Pat-thar	Stone
Paidal	On foot	Pēṙ	Tree
Pakaṙnā	To catch	Pēshāb	Urine
Pakkā	Ripe	Pēshāb *k.*	To pass urine
Palaṅg	Bed	Pēshgī *f.*	Advance (pay)
Palṭan *f.*	Regiment	Pēṭī *f.*	Belt
Pār	Across	Phailnā *Int.*	To spread
Paṙaus	Neighbourhood	Phailānā *tr.*	To spread
Paṙausī	Neighbour	Phaṭnā	To burst
Parda	Curtain	Phal *m.*	Fruit
Parē	Beyond	Phēṅknā	To throw
Paṙhnā	To read	Phir	Again; then
Phir bhī	Even then; still	Pūchhnā	To ask
Phūl	Flower	Pukārnā *v. tr.*	To shout
Pīāla	Cup	Pul	Bridge
Pīnā	To drink	Pūlīs *f.*	Police
Pītal	Brass	Purānā	Old

Q

Qabar *f.*	Grave	Qānūn	Law
Qabrustān	Cemetery *m.*	Qarīb	Near
Qadam	Pace; step	Qarz	Debt; loan
Qaiṅchī *f.*	Scissors	Qasāī	Butcher
Qamīz *f.*	Shirt	Qasūr	Fault

Qila	Fort
Qīmat *f.*	Price; Value
Qīmtī	Valuable *adj.*
Qismat *f.*	Luck
Qulī	Coolie

R

Raddī	Unserviceable
Rāē *f.*	Opinion
Rahnā	To live; dwell
Rakhnā	To put; keep
Rasad *f.*	Supplies
Rasīd *f.*	Receipt
Rassī *f.*	Rope
Rāsta	Way
Rāt *f.*	Night
Rawāna *h.*	To set out
Rawāna *k.*	To start; despatch
Rawāṅgī *f.*	Departure
Risāla	Cavalry
Rishta	Relation
Rishtedār	Relative
Rishwat *f.*	Bribe
Roknā	To stop
Ronā	To weep
Roz	Day

S

Sabab	Reason
Sabaq	Lesson
Sach-chā	True
Sadma	Shock
Safar	Journey
Safēd	White
Safēdī *f.*	White-wash
Saiṅtīs	Thirty-seven
Sāīs	Syce
Sāl	Year
Salūk	Treatment
Samajhnā	Understand
Samjhāna	To explain
Sāmān	Things
Sāmnē	In front of
Sandūq *m.*	Box
Sāṅp	Snake
Saṙak *f.*	Road
Sarhad *f.*	Frontier
Sarkār *f.*	Government
Sochnā	To ponder; think
Sonā *v. tr.*	To sleep
Sonā	Gold
Subah *f.*	Morning
Sūjan *f.*	Swelling
Sūjnā	To swell
Sikhānā	To teach
Sīkhnā	To learn
Sīnā	To sew

Sirf	Only	Shēr	Tiger
Sīti *f.*	Whistle	Shikāyat *f.*	Complaint
Sīti bajānā	To shistle	Shor	Noise
Sarkārī	Official	Sīāhī *f.*	Ink
Sastā	Cheap	Sifārish	Recommen-dation
Sāth	With	Sūkhā	Dry
Sau	Hundred	Sūkhnā *v. Int.*	To get dried
Saudāgar	Merchant	Sūkhānā	To dry
Sawērē	Early	Sulah *f.*	Peace
Sāyā	Shade	Sunnā	To hear
Sazā *f.*	Punishment	Surāgh	Clue
Sāzish *f.*	Conspiracy	Sūraj	The Sun
Shādī *f.*	Marriage	Sūrākh	Hole
Shahr	City	Surañg	Tunnel
Shak	Doubt	Sutlī	String
Shām *f.*	Evening		
Sharāb *f.*	Wine		

T

Tairnā	To swim	Tāñg	Narrow
Taīyār	Ready	Ţāñg *f.*	Leg
Taīyār *h.*	To be ready	Tankhwah *f.*	Pay
Tāga	Thread	Tāqat *f.*	Strength
Taqsīm *k.*	To divide	Tāqatwar	Strong
Tālā	Lock	Taklīf	Trouble
Tālāb	Tank	Taqrīban	Nearly
Talāsh *f.*	Search	Tār	Wire
Tamāsha	Sight	Taraf *f.*	Side
Tambākū	Tobacco	Tarah *f.*	Manner
Tambīh *k.*	To warn	Tārīf *f.*	Praise
Tambū	Tent	Tarīqa	Method
Tamgha	Medal	Tārīkh *f.*	Date

Tārkol	Tar
Tasdīq *f.*	Verification
Tasdīq *k.*	To verify
Tasma	Strap
Taswīr *f.*	Picture
Tēz	Fast; sharp
Thakānā	To tire
Thaknā	To be tired
Thakā hūā	Tired
Ṭhēka	Contract
Ṭhēkēdār	Contractor
Ṭhokar khānā	To stumble
Ṭhokar mārnā	To kick
Thūknā	To spit
Ṭika	Inocculation
Ṭika lagānā	To inocculate
Ṭirpāl *f.*	Tarpaulin
Ṭoknā	To challenge
Ṭokrā *m.*	Basket (large)
Ṭokrī *f.*	Basket (small)
Tolnā	To weight
Top *f.*	Gun
Ṭopī *f.*	Cap
Top Khāna	Artillery
Tořnā	To break
Ṭukřā	Piece
Tumhēň	accusative You
Ṭūṭnā	To be broken

U

Uchhālnā	To toss
Ummīd *f.*	Hope
Umr *f.*	Age
Uňchā	High
Unhēň (accusative)	Them
Ūpar	Above
Uřnā	To fly
Usē	(accusative) Him
Ustarā	Razor
Utarnā *v. Intr.*	To get down
Utanā *v. tr.*	To take off
Uthrnā *v. tr.*	To raise; to bear; to lift
Uṭhānā *v. tr.*	To rise
Uzr	Excuse

W

Wada	Promise
Waghaira	Etcetera
Wahāň	There
Wakīl or Vakīl	Pleader
Waqt	Time
Wāpas	Back
Wardī *f.*	Uniform
Warna	Otherwise
Warzish *f.*	Exercise (physical)
Wazan	Weight

Y

Yā	Or	Yaqīn	Certainty
Yahāṅ	Here	Yānī	That is to say

Z

Zạbān *f.*	Language; tongue	Zanjīr *f.*	Chain
Zabānī	Verbal	Zarūr	Surely; certainly
Zakhm	Wound	Zāt *f.*	Caste
Zakhmī	Wounded	Zēwar	Ornaments
Zālim	Tyrant	Zīāda	More
Zamānat *f.*	Bail	Zīn	Saddle
Zāmin	Surety	Zīnda	Alive
Zamīn *f.*	Land	Zulm	Tyranny

ISBN 81-7101-432-1

ISBN 81-7101-504-2

ISBN 81-7101-168-3

ISBN 81-7101-447-X

ISBN 81-7101-239-6

ISBN 81-7101-375-9

ISBN 81-7101-406-2

ISBN 81-7101-425-9

ISBN 81-7101-518-2

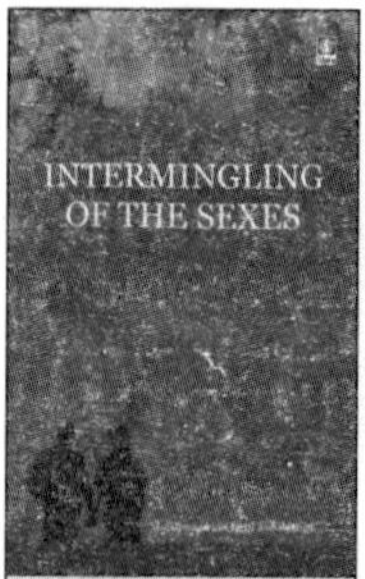

ISBN 81-7101-254-X

ISBN 81-7101-224-8

ISBN 81-7101-185-3

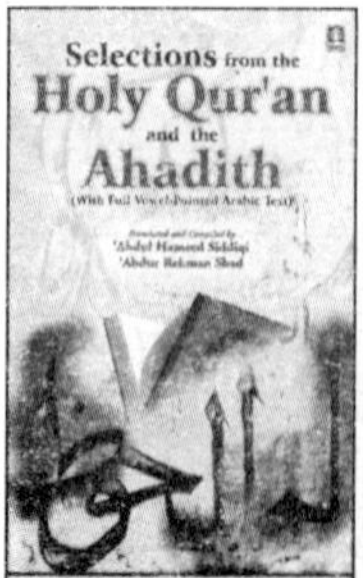

ISBN 81-7101-127-6

ISBN 81-7101-323-6

ISBN 81-7101-465-8

ISBN 81-7101-258-2

ISBN 81-7101-236-1

ISBN 81-7101-448-8

ISBN 81-7101-179-9

ISBN 81-7101-476-3

ISBN 81-7101-371-6

ISBN 81-7101-278-7

ISBN 81-7101-324-4

ISBN 81-7101-177-2

ISBN 81-7101-310-4

ISBN 81-7101-320-1

ISBN 81-7101-540-9

ISBN 81-7101-231-0

ISBN 81-7101-492-5

ISBN 81-7101-466-6

ISBN 81-7101-340-6

ISBN 81-7101-238-8

ISBN 81-7101-012-1

ISBN 81-7101-255-8

ISBN 81-7101-222-1

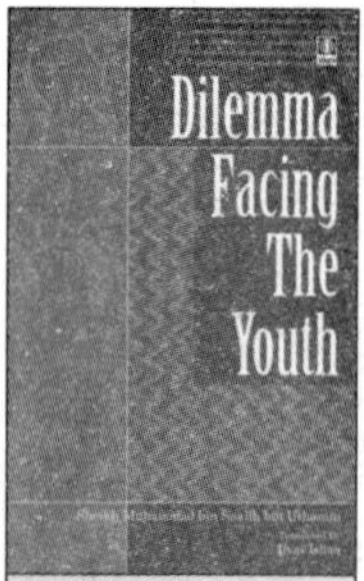

ISBN 81-7101-253-1

ISBN 81-7101-163-2

ISBN 81-7101-327-9

ISBN 81-7101-328-7

ISBN 81-7101-588-3

ISBN 81-7101-268-X

ISBN 81-7101-225-6

ISBN 81-7101-311-2

ISBN 81-7101-269-8

ISBN 81-7101-307-4

ISBN 81-7101-312-0

ISBN 81-7101-431-3

ISBN 81-7101-321-X